11/25/11

To grandson Calvin

may you enjoy

knowing my Mama

Adela

as I have enjoyed

knowing you

Love

MARY MJ

ADELA

MARY NICOL JONES

authorHOUSE®

AuthorHouse™
1663 Liberty Drive
Bloomington, IN 47403
www.authorhouse.com
Phone: 1-800-839-8640

First published by AuthorHouse   4/14/2011

ISBN: 978-1-4567-3894-5 (e)
ISBN: 978-1-4567-3895-2 (sc)

Printed in the United States of America

INTRODUCTION

My mother was known as the lady who just lies there with a lacy handkerchief over her delicate, unwrinkled face; her still dark black hair contrasting with the white pillow. Her home was now a curtained, semi-dark cubicle. The nursing home staff finally did stop trying to get her out of bed..

"She just lies there, she's lazy." Some of these efficient aides have said. What can they know of her life. "Look at her hands." Other aides have said, "You can see she is a lady, never worked hard." How little did they know about this lady, my mother..

"What do you think of when you are lying there with that lacy handkerchief over your eyes?" I asked her once.

"I go over and over my whole life," she replied.

That day on my daily visit to the nursing home, I started taking systematic notes as she repeated the many stories of her past that mama had told us when my brother and I were growing up."

Now that she is gone, now that my long vigils beside her bed are over, I can at last set down the things she remembered. Maybe the events, the emotions of those 87 years will tell why the lady with the lacy handkerchief over her face just lies there.

CHAPTER I
EARLY CHILDHOOD - NICARAGUA

My mother Adela was a baby with an auspicious beginning.

It was 1892, at Managua, Nicaragua, Central America. The street was cordoned off so that the only child of Albert Suhr and Adela Elizondo Suhr could be born in peace. This was not an unusual service provided well-to-do families. The baby was named after her mother Adela and was always called by the diminutive "Adelita," but Albert, her father called her "La Muchachita," the little girl. Her parents were typical of unions at the time, European and Latin American. In those last years of the 19th century, many European men came to Latin America to make their fortunes. Very often they married one of the eligible young women, descendants of the 17th century Spanish conquerors.

Blond, blue eyed Albert Suhr had been such a young man. He had come to United States from Germany in 1818, had studied and earned a degree in engineering at the University of Michigan. Albert became a United States citizen and had hoped to settle in North America. The young German was fluent in English, after studying the language in Germany and during his years at the University. However, soon he would need to learn a third language, Spanish.

In 1886, soon after graduation, he was offered a good position in Central America. He accepted because he felt that it would be a valuable experience, to be the Chief Engineer for the vast lands owned by a wealthy Nicaraguan family. Young Albert hated leaving the United States. He loved this free, uninhibited country. A few years later he passed that love onto his little girl, my mother Adela.

Once settled in a little town high in the mountains, which was totally owned by the Pellas family, and where he was to administer the vast lands owned by the family, he was too busy to long for that country to the North.

Albert lived on the Pellas property two years and saved every possible Cordoba, the Nicaraguan currency. He was well paid and lived comfortably, having his own house, with a patio filled with fragrant tropical plants. There were three servants, just for him, a cook, a cleaning girl, and a twelve year old girl who just did errands. However, Albert began to realize he would never be rich in his position as Chief Engineer. So after long consultation with his employers, he resigned. The Pellas family was genuinely sorry to lose him, but understood ambition very well—that is, in a white man, a non–Indian. The family offered him any help that their influence could bring.

Albert took the money he had saved and established himself in the capital, Managua. Here he started a coffee roasting business. In a year this business provided enough capital to realize his big dream, a rope factory. Until this time, rope had to be imported, and often ran short. There was plenty of hemp growing wild in the country, but no one had had the enterprise to utilize it for making rope.

So when Albert imported rope-manufacturing machinery from Germany and hired an experienced rope specialist, also from Germany, he experienced almost immediate success. The sturdy rope made from Nicaragua's plentiful hemp, sold not only there, but was exported to United States and even overseas.

He had been too busy to socialize until he was well established and his rope mill was running smoothly. But little by little he commenced meeting people and taking an interest in the social life of Managua. Then he met the beautiful Adela Elizondo, daughter of one of the socially prominent families—"la cremita" (the cream) they were called. He saw her at various social events; finally after a proper, chaperoned courtship, her huge family accepted him.

Their sumptuous, yet jubilant marriage in 1890 was one of the greatest events of the year.

A full contingent of Nicaraguan relatives attended the wedding and the magnificent reception. Adela's Aunt Matilde wore a lavender gown, closely fitted bust, corseted waist, and finally a draped flouncing skirt, white at the bottom. Tia Sulema, the melancholy aunt, dressed in grey, silver buttons cascading down her knee length tailored jacket.

The women's hats were amazing creations of a very wide, drooping brim, topped by feathers or velvet roses, others had a feathery bird on the side, and most hats had veiling cascading down the lady's back.

The gentlemen all wore coat tails, with contrasting vests and cravats tucked into the high collar of a white shirt. They held their beaver top hats underarm when they entered the church.

Music at the church was traditional, Wagner before the wedding, and Mendelssohn for the bride and groom's outgoing procession. During the ceremony both Spanish and Latin hymns filled the enormous Cathedral.

However, the music at the reception was bi-national Latin American and European. Albert insisted that Strauss, Handel, and light- hearted Humperdinck be performed. He and his stately wife followed the international custom of opening the dancing. Albert had chosen a Viennese waltz, of course. Adela held her train by a silk loop, and gently laughed when he whispered something in his Germanized Spanish.

Festivities over, the couple went to the sea town Corinto for a short honeymoon. A longer trip was out of the question. Albert had to attend to business; furthermore, he had contracted to build a huge house. In the meantime, they had rented a nice home, where his wife Adela received some of her many friends each afternoon after siesta.

The home Albert was having built took up half a square block, had two patios-one for the family, the other for the servants. It was to have every convenience. However, the new house was not completed a year later, in time for the birth of their daughter Adelita, but at least it was quiet because of the cordoned off street.

Nevertheless, six months later the family was able to move into their new home. In the rented home they had a minimum of help, but now they completed the contingent of servants every "good" family needed in that complicated, socially rigid society. There was a cook and her helper, several maids to clean, run errands, a gardener to keep the plants in the patios blooming and healthy, and of course a nana for the baby.

Albert wanted to have refrigeration in the kitchen, but he had to wait until plans to bring electricity to Managua were completed. Karl von Linden, a German, had invented refrigeration in 1876.

Nicaragua's hot, humid climate necessitated refrigeration, but it took several years for Nicaragua to have electricity. Adelita was five years old before electrification took place.

My mother's earliest recollections were of playing with her cousins the Nicols, children of her mother's sister Celia. Celia was married to Charles Samuel Nicol, who had come to Nicaragua with the British Diplomatic service. When Nicol left England he had been interested in a young lady who lived in London. At first they corresponded weekly, but when he met Celia Elizondo, Adela's sister, he broke off the relationship with the English girl. Celia was a beautiful, talented señorita. After a proper courtship he married Celia, the Nicaraguan beauty. In the following years they had six children. They were Charlie, Henry, Arthur, who was two years younger than Adelita, two girls Celia and Mary, and finally baby Dick. The Nicols and other children including Adelita played many games. One of them involved coal.

When electricity was finally installed for street lighting in Managua, the coal that had been used for lighting was discarded by the workmen. The children would bury pieces of that coal, expecting that each piece would become a diamond. Biweekly, they would dig up their "treasure," only to find the same old dirty coal.

Another game involved the sacks of coffee that had been dried and packed in sacks. Those sacks were stored in the same patios where the coffee beans had been laid out to dry.

The children climbed all over the huge heaps of coffee sacks, piled in the shape of a pyramid. The boys especially would climb to the top level, then jump from level to level, and roll on the ground as they landed on the patio. Sometimes a sack would break, spilling the beans on the floor. A workman would come screaming, "Muchachos del Diablo, tan mimados! " "Damned kids, so spoiled!"

But no one else seemed to scold them, and the potential accidents didn't seem to happen. Wild little creatures they were, left to their own devices by their pseudo-intellectual mother, Celia Nicol.

Adelita's mother, Adela Suhr was devoted to her family, but felt that if there were trouble, the nana, or some other servant would come to get her. Meanwhile, she devoted herself to her beloved Albert.

But these games soon paled for Adelita, compared to something more exciting. But first, a background of the exciting events.

In 1893, a year after my mother was born, politically turbulent

Nicaragua had been taken over by the dictator Zelaya. He brought order to the country, but at the price of terrible repression. Albert Suhr had joined his wife's party, the Conservadores. They despised the dictator, and maintained an ever active, but utterly ineffective underground.

Suhr, with his American ideas of freedom and justice, did all he could for that underground. He often suffered at the hands of Zelaya. The dictator could not touch his person because he was an American citizen. However, Zelaya could arrest his workers, and imprison and torture his wife's relatives. He went as far as attempting to deport the German-American. However, the United States consul intervened, telling the dictator that the United States would not look with favor on the maltreatment of a man who had done so much for Nicaragua. He told Zelaya,

"Mr.Suhr has established a much needed industry, the rope factory, employed hundreds and dealt fairly with them all. He would lose years of hard work if he were deported, and as yet no Nicaraguan citizen has enough experience to run his successful business."

Albert Suhr never openly opposed Zelaya, but for several years he certainly did everything in his power to help the underground. In his lovely, rambling house, he built a secret wall, hiding a room where escaped prisoners, or men being sought for arrest could be hidden till they could be spirited out of the country.

None of the servants could be trusted to know of these activities, but little Adelita, five, maybe six years old could take food to them. She was also sometimes sent with secret messages to someone in the underground. Who would suspect a child? To her it was more exciting than jumping around the coffee sacks.

How could one so young be trusted with peoples' lives? Perhaps it was her mother Adela's, aloofness and lack of attention to the child that made Adelita self-sufficient.

But to her contemporaries Adelita's mother Adela was an exciting young matron in her mid twenties, so often singing and dancing. But suddenly, my mother told me, that singing was cut short. Adela became gravely ill.

For two months Albert had helplessly watched, raged, pleaded for someone to do something about his wife's illness. It had commenced as a mild case of dysentery, became increasingly serious, simply because of lack of competent care. True, Adela's mother, large, corseted Mama Mercedes had come to the house and sat in a rocker, saying her rosary and fanning herself as she prayed for her daughter's recovery. If her life had depended on it she could never boil the clothes and bed sheets, sanitize the kitchen and the food served the patient.

Her education had not included such matters. These were for servants to carry out. But the servants were incapable of understanding sanitation; they simply blamed the devil for their mistress's condition.

Nor could Adela's younger sisters, Arcelia and Matilde be of any help. They knew how to sew, how to converse with wit, how to dress, but nursing? Ladies simply couldn't. Albert's money did him no good; there was nobody capable of taking proper care of his beloved wife. The doctor gave orders, but who could follow them. He tried to give the servants instructions. Juanita, and Rosita would say si si I understand, giggle, and when the doctor was gone so was any sanitation. .

Albert cringed when the end was near and his wife's relatives put a large lighted candle in Adelita's hands, and stood her at the foot of her mother's bed. One lone German couldn't stand against that overwhelming Spanish culture; that culture enamored of death for centuries. He was relieved, however, when the Frenchman who lived across the street, and had heard that the little girl was standing vigil at the deathbed, burst into the sick room.

He grabbed the candle out of Adelita's hands, blew it out, put his arm around her shoulders, and murmured, "Savages, savages!" Then he took her across the street to his own home.

On the first day of the new century, before her little girl was 7 years old, Adela Elizondo Suhr died. A piece of Albert died with her.

"My father's mourning was deep and terrible," my mother told me. I shivered at the thought of losing *my* mother. Then I asked, "How did you feel mama?"

She replied, "I never really felt love and physical affection from my mother, only scolding when I displeased her." I wondered if things might have changed if Adelita had had her mother Adela for a longer time.

Spanish mourning did nothing to help the little girl; She was immediately swathed in black clothing, heat of no heat. The ladies not only wore all black clothing, but draped swaths of black crepe on the front entrance, around mirrors, and on the frame of the deceased lady's portrait.

But finally mourning was toned down, and Adelita was relieved when the grandmother and aunts suggested that it was time for the little girl's First Holy Communion.

Adelita must be adequately prepared, and they recommended the child spend a year in the Assumption Convent in Lyon. This was Nicaragua's second largest city, and a cultural center. There was no satisfactory school in Managua. Adelita had attended her aunt Sulema's gentle private school. She had enjoyed the other little girls, but Albert knew she really was not receiving an adequate education. His voluminous library was evidence of his respect for learning.

So Adelita was enrolled at the Assumption convent. Here she spent one of the happiest years of her entire life. She loved and respected the gentle, dignified nuns in their purple habits. For that one year she somehow lost her undisciplined ways. It seemed peaceful to have grownups who knew what one should do, and told one so in gentle reasonable tones. They neither whined like the servants, nor shouted like her mother.

Her father never bothered with things like discipline; he simply enjoyed his "muchachita," when he was not occupied with business or his reading. Now he enjoyed his weekly visits to the convent, which took him almost a day by train. He could hardly wait for that First Communion to be done with, so he could have her back.

My mother's First Communion stayed with her all her life. To her dying day it became the core of the belief that sustained her all her life.

As soon as the school year ended, which took place a month after the First Communion, Albert requested that the nuns pack Adelita's things; she would return with him to Managua.

Many years later, when she was in the nursing home, my mother was asked how she felt on leaving the convent, where she had been so peaceful and happy. She thought a while and said, "I was disappointed of course, but I adored my father and didn't think to even want anything he didn't give me. He always gave me the things I asked for, even more than I requested. I knew how lonesome he had been while I was at the Assumption that year; over and over he said so in his long loving letters, and on his weekly visits. So it didn't occur to me to ask him to let me return to the convent."

Adelita spent the next year wandering around the huge house, reading in her father's library. She had begun to be curious about physical things, but there was no one to gently lead her into the knowledge of where babies came from, the difference between men and women, and all such things. Oh, the servants had some weird stories, and they were always snickering and whispering things she couldn't understand. Her aunts and her grandmother were no help. They felt that was a mother's duty, but there was no mother.

Furthermore, Adelita didn't know exactly what to ask. Her solution finally was in the library. She had learned to read very early from her aunt Arcelia, who had the little school, and the year at the convent had further improved her reading skills.

Eventually she found one of the medical books, with many illustrations. All alone in that cool, book lined library she learned the things a little girl almost nine should know. She also devoured Alexander Dumas, and developed a romantic sense of love from her passionate attachment to D'Artagnon, the youngest of the Three Musketeers.

When Adelita had returned to Managua she found that her English cousins had been sent to England. All Europeans sent their children to their native country to be educated. Adelita's Nicol cousins, Celia, Charley, Arthur, and even little Dick, only seven years old had lately been sent to England. But Albert was not yet ready to part with his little girl.

He worried about her, and wrote long letters to his brother Fritz in Germany. He told his brother that he was very close to his daughter, but she was getting spoiled. They always ate meals together. He would let her tell the cook what she wanted for the next meal; but when it was served, she took a bite or two, then would declare," I don't like it, the cook put too much butter, or onions, or something." He was forced to fire servants because they displeased Niña Adelita.

His brother's answering letters gave sensible advice, Adelita needed a woman's gentle care; she needed more discipline than Albert obviously was giving. But Albert could not bear to seek another wife. Then he hit on the idea of bringing that brother and the whole family to Nicaragua.

At first his brother was reluctant to leave Germany, but the more incentives Albert offered, the better it seemed. Albert would give his brother a 40% interest in his thriving business, plenty of servants, so that his wife had only to order what she wanted done, never herself have to cook or scrub. They would have their own quarters in the huge rambling house. Finally there would be the enjoyment of year round summer-no more the freezing winters of Kiel in northern Germany.

So Albert's brother Fritz and his wife packed all their belongings, outfitted the three children, Hans, Nancy, and Fritz. The family boarded the ship that took them on the long voyage through the North sea, across the Atlantic to the Caribbean and into the port of Blue Fields.

At Blue Fields they transferred to the railroad across the isthmus of Nicaragua. The Germans marveled at the modern cars, the well-kept tracks cleared of the surrounding jungle. Like all European travelers, Fritz carried his Baedeker travel guide. In it he learned that Cornelius Vanderbilt had constructed the railroad in 1850 to carry prospective gold miners to California. The future miners would disembark in Nicaragua, take the train across the isthmus, and then board another ship for California. Vanderbilt's investment paid off handsomely. The railroad was named "Accessory Transport Co." and was operated by Americans well into the 20th century.

The Suhr family received a genuine Latin welcome, a marimba band, a table loaded with food, like tortillas, quesito fresco, tamales, as well as the European dishes that Albert still preferred. He brought out his best wines, and had plenty of good imported beer. His family's first impression made them glad they had come.

As weeks passed, they still had to admit that the picture Albert had painted of hordes of servants, of a wonderful big house, of warm sunny days, were all true. But also true was the utter ignorance of the servants, their stubborn refusal to follow the sanitary methods his sister-in-law, their new mistress, tried to teach them. The eternal summer was actually an oppressive heat, necessitating change of clothing several times a day.

A mother could not be everywhere at once. She could not catch the servants sneaking messy, dirty sweets to her little blonde children, against strict orders. Nor could a parent, in spite of every precaution, nets, clothing to cover exposed skin, prevent a child from being bitten by mosquitoes. Finally, Albert in his glowing tales of Nicaragua could not have foreseen the tragedy that caused his dear family to pack their bags, arrange for passage to Germany and never return to that accursed country. The victim of this tragedy was his brother's middle child, little Nancy, just five years old.

At first Nancy seemed just listless, then her stomach began to swell. The doctors diagnosed Filariasis, caused by Mosquitoes. They prescribed one medicine after another, then finally a complete fast.

My mother recalls the little girl pleading for food, finally crying "Just one little grain of rice, I promise I wont ask for more." She never got her grain of rice, and within three days, Nancy was dead.

There was no argument left in Albert. With resignation he agreed with his brother that Adelita should be educated in Germany. But his wife would not wait until their niece Adelita could be prepared.

Besides, no arrangements had been made for schooling, or a place to live. His wife was too upset to take on the added burden of a half-wild little girl. She felt Adelita was partially schooled, and did not even speak German.. The relatives departed with a promise to look for a good school and suitable living arrangements.

Actually, Albert's little girl had been to Germany when she was four. Albert had taken his wife, Adela to Germany for an operation on a lame leg, caused by a boil. She had refused to have it tended and it had eaten its way through the bone and made the leg shorter. Albert and Adela decided that they would take their four year old daughter Adelita with them.

My mother vividly remembered the long ocean voyage across the Atlantic, into the North Sea, and finally the docking at Kiel, in Germany. Memories of the trip to Kranz, the small town where her grandmother lived were vague. However, she remembered the large woman who couldn't speak Spanish, but hugged her and right away offered her a cookie.

The little girl stayed with her grandparents for six months, while her parents went to Berlin for the operation. In those months, she forgot her Spanish, and couldn't communicate with her mother when she returned from Berlin. However, as children can so easily do, she soon relearned Spanish, and proceeded to forget her German. Too bad she had forgotten her baby German, now that she was to reenter her father's native land.

I asked my mother, when I sat by her bed at the nursing home, how she had felt going to a strange country, no language, no friends; she replied, "Scared, I guess." Mama continued, "Events just happened to me in my early life. They put a candle in my hands when my mother was dying, I just stood there till rescued by the nice Frenchman who rushed in. I was so relieved!." Mama went on, "I loved the convent, but Papa was lonesome, so I went home with him. Then they all decided I should go to Germany, though a little frightened, I was excited about learning new things. The hours I spent in Papa's library, made me long for more knowledge, more understanding."

But this time the change in her life was good, as near to normal as the year in the convent had been. Those four years in Germany were to mold her character more than the years in Nicaragua.

Most acquaintances, including my brother and I were to think of her more German than Spanish.

CHAPTER II -
GERMANY

Now Albert began making arrangements for his eleven year old daughter's trip to Germany. He learned that a trusted friend of the family, Alfredo Whelock, was making a business trip to Germany When Albert approached him, Whelock said he would be glad to see that Adelita got safely to her relatives in Kiel, where most of the family lived.

Letters went back and forth to the whole family, to his mother, to his brothers, including Fritz who had come to Nicaragua but left when his little girl Nancy died. He also wrote to his sister, who had married very well, a Mr. Feldmann. The Feldmanns lived in a spacious house in Kiel, had a large family, and surely would interest themselves in his muchachita.

The Nicaraguan aunts took charge of outfitting the little

girl with what was worn in Germany. There was underwear and many sets of skirts and middy blouses. They also hired a skilled shoemaker to make some sturdy shoes. The ladies shivered at the thought of their little neice out of dainty feminine slippers and into those dreadful shoes; they looked like boats!

Finally the day of departure arrived; Mr.Whelock, his young charge and Albert climbed into the buggy that took them to the railroad station. The three boarded the train that was to cross the Isthmus of Nicaragua. One last embrace and Albert descended to the platform, where he sadly waved as the train slowly pulled away. I can imagine that he did not try to stop the tears as the train disappeared and he likely wondered what his little girl was thinking.

As she sat in the plush seat next to the window, Adelita wished she had kept the German learned as a little child. Oh well, she would learn it again. Meantime she practiced her numbers in German to the clickety clack of the train; eine, zwei, drei, vier, funf.

It was a long trip across the Isthmus, across the Atlantic veering ever north, finally docking at Kiel.

Adelita enjoyed the voyage and the attention adults paid her. Even proper businessman Mr. Whelock brushed her long black hair every morning. She complained that the stewardess assigned them didn't do it right. But as she disembarked with Mr. Whelock Adelita did not have the slightest idea what to expect. But there to her delight and surprise, the wonderful, serious relatives were all standing on the dock. They knew the little girl from "Amerika" didn't know German; so they had learned a few Spanish words. Adelita tried not to giggle at their funny accent but really appreciated their efforts.

However, Adelita, soon to be called Adela, a more sensible name for an eleven-year-old madchen—was shocked and humiliated when she found where she was to live. First, the spacious apartment where she was to have room and board with Frau Kensler and her two daughters was over a grocery store. Second, Frau Kensler had been a cook, at one of the most prestigious estates in Kiel, but a cook nevertheless. In Latin America the young people of "gente" families never went near the kitchen, nor fraternized with servants.

"When I complained to my relatives," mama explained to me "they somehow managed to explain to me that my father had wanted to be sure I had someplace where I would eat healthful food." Mama explained that when they wrote to him that the cook of some rich people had retired, but wanted to have a boarder, he thought it was a good place for his daughter—she would be well fed.

"Papa was lost to the social subtleties of Latin America, like one did not live in close quarters with servants," Mama explained. But she couldn't answer why one of the relatives didn't have her in their own home. She seemed to just accept things.

But my mother finally made the best of it. With help of a dictionary she tried to communicate with Frau Kistler, her daughters and of course with her relatives. Educated Europeans, including Germans, knew several languages; but Spanish was not deemed important, unless one needed it for business. Everyone assured Adela she would quickly master the language when she started her new school that next week.

Although she could not communicate with the young ladies at the exclusive academy where her relatives had enrolled her, she immediately liked the school and her fellow students. She felt they were her own kind, although very plainly dressed, and all so very blond. The girls were friendly and seemed fascinated by the young foreigner with the long black hair and the large, sad, questioning eyes.

The first three months were the most difficult, trying to understand the lessons, although she did have private tutoring. Often two or three girls would come up to her,"Adela, let us help you." Hilda, who knew a word or two of Spanish said, "Facile, facile el Aleman." Then they all giggled and slowly pronounced word after German word, which Adela slowly repeated.

After three months, the German she had learned as a baby girl on that first trip came back. Her tongue could manage the deep-throated consonants. She was excused from English class—obligatory for the others—because one new language was enough with which to struggle.

This country was so different from Nicaragua, but Adela loved the orderliness of the Germans. Between each class the students were obliged to go outside and told to play vigorously, even in winter. Out they went, for ten minutes—exactly. On returning to the classroom, the students were alert, as their elders had planned. She was learning so much; my mother never forgot the poetry she was taught. Nor did she forget her "friendship" with authors Schiller and Goethe.

Years later, when my brother and I were little she used to take us to Golden Gate Park, where there was a statue of these two great

German writers. I almost felt they were relatives, with such affection did my mother speak of them. She knew so many poems—I still have an audiotape of my mother reciting in her lovely soft German, Di Elkoinig, the Glocke by Schller and many others.

In summer the girls would go to one of the long sandy beaches along the Kiel Canal; there they would study together. Several girls invited her home; however, she was never able to reciprocate. She was ashamed of her "home" over the grocery store.. The girls felt sorry for her, and thought how horrible of her relatives to put her to live with those so beneath her. My mother couldn't explain why but just accepted things as they were.

Only in summer, when the family gathered at Blanquenaise, grandmama's home, did she feel totally accepted. She felt loved by them all, especially cousin Albert, three years older, who would tease her and give brotherly advice.

Summer over Adela returned to Frau Kensler's and school. No more language trouble, she was able to chat and gossip with her schoolmates. Adela was puzzled why the German girls didn't approve of her friendship with some of the girls who were Jewish. In Nicaragua there were Jewish families, Tefels, Berheims. Some had become Catholic, but ethnically they remained Jewish. Why did the German girls, so nice to her a foreigner, completely ostracize the Jewish girls? When she asked, their only explanation was "The Jews have always been a problem." That ended the discussion.

Though she lived four miles from the school, summer was no problem. She rode her bicycle, and was there in no time. But winter was horrible. Adela had to walk the four miles. That entire winter she would have a cough. So bad, in fact, that they would send her back home, through the snow! She well could have died of pneumonia. Mama did have weak lungs the rest of her life.

But summers made up for all the winter misery. Four summers were spent at her grandmother's home in Blankenese down the Elbe canal from Kiel. She felt loved, by her grand parents, Meta and Albert Suhr senior and her cousin, Albert Felddman. Albert was the eldest son of her father's only sister Matilde Felddman. The senior Suhrs had four boys but Matilde was their only girl. Young Albert would give Adela advice, seeing he *was* three years her senior.

During these summer visits, Adela's grandfather Albert Senior would take Adela on trips on his ferry boat, down the Elbe. She was entranced by his tales of how he had made his fortune in the early 1850's.

Mama years later told the story to us that her grandfather had told her.

GRANDFATHER ALBERT SUHR

My grandfather Albert senior had an independent nature, eternally rebelling against the rigid discipline inherent in the German social system. He heard of the gold discoveries in America and longed to go to California. He fancied a lovely young lady in Kiel, but was too young and without means to think of marriage.

His mother had money put away and gave him enough to book passage to California.

First there was the long trip across the cold Atlantic, and second the arrival at the steaming tropical port of Blue Fields, Nicaragua. Here he boarded a train across the Central American peninsula, and then onto a second ship, which finally docked at San Francisco. Here he found other Germans who showed him the fundamentals of finding gold. The stories told all over the world about gold to be panned in the rivers of the Sierras were true. There was even a German Sea chantey about the "Banks of the Sacramento."

Young Albert did well in the gold fields. He prudently had the precious metal boxed and stored, instead of selling it to the often dishonest dealers around assay offices and banks. When he felt he had amassed a sufficient fortune to return a rich man and try for the hand of the girl he loved, he booked passage for Holland. Here he would get a better price for his boxes of gold. His planning proved wise, for when he left Holland for Kiel, he had a sizeable bank draft in his portfolio.

He found his sweetheart still single and very interested in the attentions of the exciting young Suhr boy. When Meta said yes to his proposal and he had formally asked for her hand, he commenced making plans for the future.

In anticipation of their marriage, my Grandfather Albert commissioned the building of what was to be one of the grandest houses in Kranz.

At the same time the bride's family prepared for a true German wedding. At this time weddings were Wagnerian spectacles! Many of the customs were descended from Germanic tribes, like the custom of bread and salt given the couple at the wedding feast, or like the horses either black or white, to draw the wedding carriage.

Arrangements were made for the Lutheran church near their home. Even before Meta's wedding dress and trousseau were complete the bride went with her father to choose the horses that would pull her wedding carriage. Meta chose two black Holsteiner stallions. After that she went back to a fitting for her bridal gown of heavily embroidered material. She would wear the traditional crown, covered by a veil of again intricately embroidered fabric.

When finally all was ready, the night before the wedding, the wild Polterbend (evening uproar) took place. This too was passed down from the tribes. All the young men who were to take part in the wedding gathered outside to make a huge noise. They cracked whips, shot guns, and smashed basketfuls of crockery. They laughingly explained to any one passing by, " We want to Kaput the evil spirits." No doubt their tribal ancestors were watching and cheering.

But the wedding ceremony and the reception were dignified and very serious. Meta and Albert were joined in wedlock for life, a life that brought them three boys and a girl. Albert, Fritz Tony, and Matilde.

After the wedding Albert continued working on plans he had commenced months earlier.

He had negotiated the purchase of a large cargo/passenger ferryboat. There were other boats on the Elbe canal transporting passengers, as well as fruit and produce grown on the farms near Kiel and taken to ports along the Elbe Canal. However, the owners of these other boats were casual and kept no schedule. The practical young Albert disapproved of their manner of doing business, but kept his peace until after the wedding.

Finally he called a meeting of all ferryboat owners. The gruff older men convened at Albert's magnificent house, were treated to the best beer, wine and food, and at last were seated to hear what was on young Suhr's mind.

Respectfully, but with total self-assurance, the young man proposed that the ferry owners set up a regular schedule. Thus shippers and passengers could count on a time of departing and arrival. They heard him out, but one after another threw the age-old arguments elders give the young. "It has always been done this way; we would lose money going before the boat is full. You young fellows always think you know more." And on and on.

So Albert threw his trump card. Either they agreed to his proposal or he would run his ferry free. Looking around, they knew he could afford to keep his threat. So one by one the men agreed. The association they formed that day prospered and drew business from far up and down the Elbe. Farmers could plan to have their produce to market in time; businessmen could plan a day in Kiel or Hamburg and know when they could return home.

Besides listening to his stories and having the wonderful trips on his ferry Adela also played with the village children. She became the wild child she had been in Nicaragua when she played with her Nicol cousins.

The boys especially would tease her and call her "Indianeren" from Amerika. Adela would take off a wide belt she wore, and lash out at them.

They ran back home, terrified; that terrible Indian from America! Cousin Albert was on a summer trip, or surely would have told Adela she must be more ladylike.

But there was another boy who did not scold or tease her. Adela met Herbert when the young people were watching a circus—as paying customers? Mama never explained. Besides meeting at the circus, Adela and Herbert used to go bicycling together. It wasn't quite proper for a boy and a girl to go traipsing around all alone. When she told Frau Kensler Herbert's last name, Vright, the good lady raised her hands and exclaimed, "That's the son of the people I worked for. Oh he is very rich, but such a nice boy. They are good people, who never spoil their children."

She further elaborated and told Adela, "Their estate is enormous. They fenced off the portion near their mansion, but the rest they left open, allowing the public to use it as a park. Anyone can walk by the beautiful lake, and down the well kept paths. Visitors can smell the Lilacs and listen to the multitude of birds in a variety of trees."

On some of their bicycle rides Adela and Herbert went to the estate, but stopped at the coachman's house. The wife would give them cookies and a glass of milk and admonish Herbert to get Adela home before dark. Not that there was any crime to fear, but just that a young lady must get home for dinner at a proper hour. "Of course" Herbert would say, "I myself have to be home for dinner, promptly."

On weekends Herbert would come for Adela and they would go together to visit his "poor people." He had a good allowance, and most of it went to helping people he had discovered were in some sort of trouble—a widow with a sick baby, a man who had broken his leg and couldn't work.

Frau Kensler never scolded Adela for being with Herbert because she was impressed that the girl had made friends with such an illustrious person. Romance? During the four years that Adela was in school here, they were just children. The nearest Herbert ever came to even touch Adela was when he would push her bike as they came to a hill. Yes, these were happy years, even in spite of the snow and the winter coughs. During the four years that she was in school here, Adela and Herbert just enjoyed being young.

These had been four satisfying years but the first part of the German Educational system was finished. Adela would have to change schools or return home. She did not give much thought to her future. The young lady was enjoying one last summer at her grandmother's house in the country, Blanquenese.

* * * * * * * *

* * * * * *

"All this was happening at this time in your early life. How did you feel Mama, what did you want?"

"I had no power to question the decisions made for me - decisions like being sent back through the snow when I coughed too much; decisions about my continued education. I just accepted what the adults decided."

* * * * * * *

Meanwhile, Albert Suhr, her father and Charles Samuel Nicol, his brother-in-law were discussing the possibilities of the young lady finishing her schooling in England.

CHAPTER III
England & Return to Nicaragua

Albert liked Charles Nicol who was married to his wife Adela's sister Celia. However, he considered his sister-in-law a silly, pretentious woman. Mrs. Nicol insisted that she and her husband stand on a slight dais to greet guests at the soirees they hosted-silly ostentation, he thought.

But the practical German enjoyed Nicol when they were man to man. It was just such an occasion when they met in the cool patio of Suhr's home to discuss Adelita's future. Both men had blue eyes, and sported full mustaches, curled at the ends. Only Nicol had a beard, a well trimmed goatee.

The men agreed that the four years in Germany were not enough to consider a young woman truly educated. As they sat and talked, Charles proposed a solution. He leaned toward his friend Albert and said "I am planning a trip to England to check in with the Foreign Office, and of course to see my Children in school. If one of the German relatives could take Adelita to England, I would see that she was enrolled in a proper girls' academy.."

Albert remembered how his little daughter had loved the convent in Granada, so he suggested that maybe a convent in England might be good. Charles agreed with Albert, but his staunch Protestant soul silently shivered at the thought of a "Papist" institution; but he kept his thoughts to himself. Instead he suggested Albert write his relatives requesting that one of them take Adelita to England and temporarily leave her at Miss Rose's School in London. The youngest Nicol children, Dick and Celia were enrolled there. Once in England it would be decided where she would continue her schooling.

After receiving a letter from Albert in Nicaragua, the German relatives convened to discuss who should take her to England, what clothes would be appropriate; should they try to teach her a few words of English? The young girl had nothing to say, but was mildly excited about the new life that awaited her.

Uncle Adolf, who had business in London, volunteered to take Adela to England. Her excitement grew as the new clothes were packed, she practiced some English words. Ya, these new words feel like German.

Finally all was ready and Adolf and Adela boarded a train to Cherbourg, transferred to a small ship to England, and finally boarded another train to London. Here they took a carriage to the Victorian style house that was Miss Roses' Elementary Academy. Adela's mounting excitement turned to apprehension as they walked up the marble steps..

Adolf rang the bell, and when Hans, the German butler opened it and greeted them, Adolf asked to see Miss Rose, but was told she was unavailable at the moment. However, Hans assured Adolf that he would take care of the young lady. So her uncle bid Adela goodbye with a handshake and went back to the waiting carriage.

At first Hans spoke in English, but when he realized Miss Suhr didn't understand, he switched to German. He conducted her to a small room, where he told the young lady to unpack, and freshen up in time for Tea at four o'clock. He promised to come for her and take her to the dining room. Here she would meet Miss Rose.

The butler was as good as his word and promptly at five minutes to four, Adela was escorted down stairs and entered the dining room. She had waited only moments, when a thin, long faced woman, dressed in black, with a high neck lace collar, entered the room and extended her long well manicured hand; "Welcome Miss Suhr." Then she added a few German words, and concluded, "You will have to learn English, before you can go to another school." Adela felt a mixture of excitement and apprehension, until she was distracted by the appearance of a group of children coming into the dining room.

Among the youngsters coming in for tea, Adela immediately recognized Celia Nicol. In Latin fashion they embraced and chattered in Spanish—this time Adela had not forgotten her original language. Miss Rose looked askance at the two girls, but said nothing. Then Celia beckoned to a small boy, who was about to be seated at the oblong table covered with a lace cloth and set with dainty cups.

"Adelita, this is Dick." He bowed politely, "Glad to see you, cousin." The baby boy Adela remembered had become a proper English lad. In fact that weekend, when the older boys who were enrolled at Cheltham, came for a visit, she was amazed that the wild undisciplined boys with whom she had played in Nicaragua had become young English Gentry. All three boys, Charley, Henry, and Arthur wore proper suits, high collared shirts, and stood in straight military fashion. All three kept their hands clasped behind the back, when not in use.

The next day a routine was established. Adela was installed in the dining room. There was no other place for her to study, because she was too old to attend classes for the children.

She was given English lessons when one of the teachers had no class. Also, she was presented with all the books she wanted to read. At first simple children's stories, then as her English improved, some English literature as well as world history. Among the authors she read were Robert Louis Stevenson, Thomas Hardy, Rudyard Kipling and a return to her beloved The Three Musketeers, this time in English.

However, there was no one her age with whom she could talk. For hours she sat in the dining room. Then sometimes, when he came to set the tables for the next meal, she would talk to the German butler. He brought back memories of Germany, especially when he passed plates of food to the children at meals. He would click his heels and say "Bitte", that all encompassing German word that translates "Please", but can mean "Excuse me" "Please have some", etc. etc.

Seven months passed by and she became increasingly bored and then angry. At least she did have the consolation that she had mastered fluent English, and learned a great deal about England. She had proper Tea Time manners; and participated in the weekly dance lessons, at least she watched, because she could not possibly partner with the little boys half her size. Also, she learned that the English, at least in boarding schools, did not believe in overeating. In fact she and the children were often hungry when they went to bed. Were it not for two kindly spinster ladies who lived next door and handed the children food through a window that was close to one of the dormitories, they would have been hungry every single night. Those little boarders never forgot the dear Geiken sisters.

Finally, seven months later Adela received a letter from her father in which he explained why she had not been settled into the right school. He explained that Charles Samuel Nicol, who was supposed to have made the arrangements for her when he came to England had to cancel his trip several times because he was ill. Charles always had digestive problems, but each time a bout of severe stomach pain incapacitated him, he would send word to Suhr that his trip must be delayed. The third time this happened, seven months after Adela had been taken to England, Charles told his brother-in-law Albert that perhaps he had better send for his daughter.

So it was that Albert cabled a Nicaraguan associate, who was in England on business, asking him to bring his daughter Adelita back to Nicaragua when he returned. Don Gustavo Santiago wired back; he would be delighted to escort the young lady on the trip to Nicaragua. His wife had joined him in England and they planned to return home via New York. If Albert would wire some money, they would be glad to take Adelita shopping in that city.

Adela was disappointed that she would not have further

schooling in England, but getting out of that dining room was a huge relief. Don Santiago and his wife called on her at Miss Rose's, and together they made plans for the trip back to America.

RETURN TO NICARAGUA

The children were sorry to see the "big girl" leaving. She was always kind to them, and helped with arithmetic sometimes. Those arithmetic sessions had been a help for her "pupils", but more of a relief to Miss Suhr, She could at least once in a while talk to SOMEone.

Miss Rose was even almost pleasant as she said in parting, "I wish you well my dear; don't forget England and the English language." Adela never did forget English; she had no accent, just a touch of German in her pronunciation—like "duc" for dock. Oh, how we children used to tease her!

When her clothes were all packed and ready for the trip to America, the Santiagos called for Adela and took her to their hotel for one night. They were to board ship early in the morning. Albert had wired a generous sum of money, with a request that Adela be outfitted in appropriate clothes for Nicaragua, when they were in New York.

The trip across the Atlantic did not seem long because there were so many interesting people with whom to converse. The Santiagos, of course, spent many hours telling her all about Nicaragua, who was grown up now, what was happening politically—the American Marines had become an important part of their lives. My mother became "Adelita" again, and would always be to her Spanish relatives and friends.

Besides the Santiagos, she met and spent some happy times with a German family, who had a daughter and son close to her age. The young people would sit on deck and sing German songs, clapping hands when they sang a march.

Then there was an English lady, who invited Adela to tea a few times. Mrs. Flintridge was amazed that her young friend had learned so much English in just seven months in England. So on this voyage, this young woman, my mother became more proficient in the three languages she had acquired in her fifteen years.

The ship finally landed in New York, where the bustle of landing, customs, and settling in at their hotel took a couple of days. Then Mr. and Mrs. Santiago needed to attend to the important procedure of shopping. To well- to-do Latin Americans, shopping in the States is like religion. When they return home, friends and relatives will not rest till they have seen everything that was brought from "Los Estados Unidos." Adelita's shopping was turned over to the concierge, who offered to take the young lady to buy whatever she might need. Mr. Santiago gave the concierge $500 to cover the purchases.

After spending the day visiting various shops and department stores, more than half the money was unspent. Adelita had chosen exactly two dresses, one pair of pretty shoes, a pair of stockings and one hat. The concierge asked, "Is this all you want, dear?" "Yes" she replied, I don't need anything more."

The Santiagos were too busy packing up their own purchases and gifts to take home to look into what Adelita had purchased. Furthermore, they had no authority to insist that Adelita buy more. Mr. Santiago merely changed the remaining money into a

Nicaraguan Cordoba letter of credit, which he stowed in the small safe he brought with him on all his trips.

However, when she arrived home to Managua, Nicaragua no such hands off attitude greeted the practical Adelita. The Aunts and Uncles and cousins did not appreciate her German thrift. They were shocked at the meager result of her American shopping trip. The aunts hired two dressmakers to properly outfit what was considered an adult young lady—A young lady who would appear in society at fifteen, as the finished product of a European education!

The dressmakers made simple cotton dresses for the morning, more elaborate gowns for the afternoon, for calling, or shopping, or walking in the plaza. There were dresses just right for trips to the coast, but most important were the gowns for the balls she would attend.

Adelita's first dance reception was in 1908 at the American Embassy, hosted by the Major General of the U.S. Marine troops. The Marines had been sent by President Theodore Roosevelt to oust the dictator Zelaya. This was the tyrant that Albert Suhr had despised, and opposed secretly, and that as part of that opposition had allowed his little daughter to carry messages to the underground.

My mother enjoyed her first ball, and was very popular with the tall American officers. They were intrigued at the Nicaraguan girl with the British accent. But balls and other social events with the Americans and with her own people did not make up for the changes in her father's life.

While Adelita was in Germany, he had married her mother

Adela's middle sister, Rosalia. She was a gentle young woman, who would have taken a loving interest in her stepdaughter. However, before Adelita returned from Germany, just a year and a half after her marriage to Albert, she died in childbirth. Her child, a boy did not survive.

After a year of once again mourning a wife, Albert married the youngest of the Elizondo girls, Matilde. It was a disaster. She was much too young for the middle aged German, very stupid and ignorant, and incapable of dealing with her two little boys in any way but hitting them on the head when they displeased her.

Albert escaped in drink, and often humiliated Adelita by scenes in public.

Once when they were returning from a visit in the evening, he stopped the carriage, jumped out, and staggered up to the door of a house of ill repute. He banged on the door and denounced the "dirty" goings on. Adelita loved her father's strict morality, but this was no way to demonstrate that morality. So three years after returning, at age nineteen, she finally decided to accept her cousin Sarita's pleas to come to Paris.

This cousin had been staying at the Nicaraguan Embassy in the French capital for six months. She kept sending letters begging Adelita to come join her; she was having such a glorious time.

Also, Adelita had, these three years in Nicaragua, received letters from Germany. Her relatives would so love to see her again. Especially interesting was correspondence from Albert Feldmann, the cousin three years her senior who had given her brotherly advice when they met at family gatherings. He wrote urging her to visit. He told her that if she stopped in Paris and assembled a fashionable wardrobe, he would escort her to the best places in Kiel and Hamburg. She begged her father to let her take the trip. As usual anything his muchachita wanted was his command.

So it was she booked passage for France, with a final stop at Paris. Further plans for the trip to Germany, Adela would arrange during her time in France.

CHAPTER IV
BACK TO GERMANY _VIA PARIS

Once again Adela crossed the Atlantic, but this time heading for Cherbourg, France. She had made friends with a German couple, Hans and Gertrude Frieberg, on the trip across. They were heading for Paris. When the three young people had boarded the train from Cherbourg and settled themselves into the compartment they would share for the short trip to Paris, they all chatted about what Adela might expect from her stay at an embassy. They predicted good times, and Gertrude gave Adela tips on the best couturiers for the wardrobe she planned to acquire during her stay.

The young German woman had been to Paris many times, and rattled off names like Vionnet, Paul Poiret, Chanel, and Schiaparelli. When the train pulled into the Paris station, Adela parted company with the Friebergs with promises to see them during their stay. The Embassy had sent a coach for Adela, and soon she was on her way with her luggage piled on top of the conveyance.

When she arrived at the Embassy, an elegant building, fronted by a portico with Doric columns; standing there were her cousin and several people whom she would learn to know and love in the months ahead.

Adelita was soon settled because a maid had been assigned to help her unpack and place her things either in the huge armoire, or in the drawers of a carved bureau with a huge gold framed mirror above it. She was escorted downstairs and into one of the luxurious salons. Her cousin chattered on and on about the plans she had for Adelita. The visitor would soon see why her cousin Sarita had been begging her to come.

Don Eduardo Tefel, the Ambassador, was well acquainted in Paris. He had been educated in France, and his wife had attended the Sacre Coeur in Paris. Monsieur L'Ambassedeur was handsome and of quick wit, so he was included at the most prestigious gatherings.

So Adelita's first month was a round of teas, parties, and art exhibits. Picasso, Matisse, Juan Gris were gaining fame and had been included at Gertrude Stein's salons. The Nicaraguans liked the work of the first two artists, but cubist Gris they found strange." His paintings are not pretty!" Young ladies would giggle.

What Adelita most enjoyed was the Ballet Russe, which had just come to Paris from Russia. But after a month she asked her cousin to help her accomplish the task her worldly cousin Albert, in Germany, had assigned her—to create a wardrobe appropriate for the life style to which he would introduce her.

Adelita knew by heart the names of the leading couturiers. From among ateliers Worth, Doucet, Paquin, Schiaparelli, she finally chose Paul Poiret. Both Adelita and her cousin Sarita liked the creations they saw at one of his shows.

I have no photographs of the gowns, suits and hats that were created for her and made at Poiret's establishment . I do recall, though, some of the descriptions my mother gave me.

Poiret had "loosened the corset," he liked the natural female shape. One gown I recall my mother describing had a full skirted over blouse, reaching midcalf. It was silk, printed in brilliant colors. Poiret was greatly influenced by China and the Far East. The underskirt of the garment was black, and draped to a peak above the ankles.

One of her favorites was a tailored suit.. The skirt ended just above the ankle, and the jacket, with a Russian collar, reached to just below the hips. The sensational touch, however, were the buttons that went from the collar, down the side of the jacket, then on the skirt, all the way to the hem.

There were many other creations for her wardrobe that my mother remembered. However, the coat, full skirted, and trimmed at the bottom with Lynx fur, sounded sensational to me.

My mother told how the clients had to be taught to walk in the narrow skirts originated by Poiret, "Hobble skirts" they were called. That creation of his did not last long—walking, even with expert instruction, was near to impossible.

The wardrobe, of course, included many hats. One I remember my mother describing. It had a medium size brim, with Egret feathers cascading from the side of the face to below the shoulder. Egret feathers became outlawed years later. Feathers were plucked from live birds. I am sure my mother didn't know of the terrible cruelty that had produced her hat.

When her wardrobe was complete, the girls became busy with travel plans. Sarita was to return to Nicaragua, where eventually she married a very wealthy young man who had begged for her hand for several years. She finally decided the Paris frivolous life offered no future. She wrote the young man that she was returning home. My mother made arrangements to return at last to Germany.

She chose train travel to Kiel. There she was greeted not only by cousin Albert, but by numerous cousins, aunts, uncles and their friends. They thought of her more arriving from Paris, than from her native land. My mother told me many stories of those years, the happiest times in her life.

It was 1912. Little did she imagine what would await her and the world in two years, two beautiful years she would tell us about over and over.

GERMANY I912 TO 1914

As Adela descended from the train, and saw her cousins, she recalled that there had been Latin American cousins at home and recently in Paris. Now the German cousins were before her. She realized that she was half Spanish half German **Adela/Adelita!**

But when she told me of those two years in Germany she seemed mostly German, and that's how I usually thought of mama.

So there they stood at the Kiel train station—Fritz, Herman,

Josey, Albert, the eldest and their mother Matilde. There were not the hugs and squeals like her Latin relatives, instead a very loving embrace and those left cheek, right cheek kisses born in Europe. They all piled into a large gasoline powered conveyance, which they had hired. As soon as the driver had loaded Adela's luggage in the back part, including eight hat boxes, the conveyance roared off to Kranz where cousin Albert and his parents lived in the house Albert Suhr Senior, the grandfather had built. It had stood the years well, since he returned from the gold fields of California. His daughter Matilde and her husband Albert Feltmann had made a few improvements, but the mansion had stood solid all these years.

When they entered, the scent of coffee and strudel that had been prepared by the maid greeted them. Almost immediately they were seated at the elaborately carved table where they chatted away for a couple of hours.

The conversation commenced with questions about Nicaragua. "Are there many Germans there?" asked lively young Fritz.

"Yes." Adela replied, "In fact, there is a thriving German club, which my father insisted I join, so as to keep up my German. Also, he hoped I would meet a nice German young man and-----." she blushed, " well, marry."

"Did you?" chuckled Herman, the middle son, who sported a small mustache. "No, but I was annoyed by a Herr Bunje, a prosperous man, ten years my senior. Father thought he would be a good match." They all laughed at the sour face she made.

Then the talk turned to politics. Albert spoke of the dangers he foresaw. His deep blue eyes flashed, "That devil Baron Fritz von

Holstein, he hates Russia, and could ruin the years our leaders have spent, not exactly making friends with Russia but at least containing her ambitions."

"Our dear Kaiser," added Herman "He is a good monarch, but has so little experience in statesmanship."

"And the Balkan situation," added Albert "they have chopped Bulgaria in three parts, and Bosnia and Herzegovina, the former Turkish provinces, given to Austria to administer. They never consulted the people who live there, no one considered the ethnic realities..

The family finally ended the lively coffee session with a list of the plans they had for their visitor. One was to be a ride on the ferry that Albert Suhr, their grandfather had purchased when he returned from California. Adela remembered that when she was in school here, her grandfather had taken her on the run to Kiel, and had even let her take the wheel when there was not any visible traffic. She said to her cousins, "Yes, I would so love to see the ferry again, and have a little trip on it. Next Aunt Matilde spoke of their Rathweinkellar. "We are so proud of it Adela." But before she said any more, Albert took his cousin's arm and led her into the parlor.

"I am anxious to show you our Rathweinkellar." He explained that most German cities had a restaurant in the cellar of the courthouse. His father had purchased the one at the Kiel courthouse. It was frequented by interesting people—professors, members of the government, stage celebrities from opera and drama. Even the young princes often came. "In fact, Adela, I must warn you. Never never flirt with one of the princes. If one of them should be attracted to you, he would feel he had a right to have you. I would have to fight a duel to protect your honor."

So it was that Adela was prim and proper when two days later Albert escorted her to the Rathweinkellar. The Maitre de greeted them enthusiastically, he had heard so much from Albert, and from his employer, Albert's father, about the cousin from Amerika. When they were seated in a comfortable booth, overlooking much of the main room, it soon filled with chatting, laughing men and women in evening attire. Albert leaned toward Adela and whispered, "You are the most elegant frauline here." And Adela chuckled in satisfaction; her laughing eyes told him, 'I know! '

The Keller reflected the ancient German culture. Huge sanded and oiled beams, which were of course necessary as they supported the two-story courthouse above, were at the length and breadth of the two rooms. The wooden walls held paintings of ancient tribes, warring, rejoicing, all exuding great strength. But these descendants of ancient Germans had absorbed the elegance of Rome, which had absorbed the sophistication of Greece. There were crystal wine glasses on crisp white table clothes, and attentive waiters, well versed in International gourmet food and the great wines of France, Italy, and of course the mellow, complicated white wines of Germany.

Years later, in the nursing home, my mother asked me "Mary, I wish I could have a small bottle of a good German wine." I asked the head nurse," Is it possible for my mother to have a little bottle or two of white wine." She replied that several of the patients, with their doctor's permission could have a small supply of one glass bottles, kept in a locker, and served with dinner.

When I had the doctor's permission, I went to Beltramo's, a top wine merchant and purchased four bottles of a good German wine recommended by the wine buyer.

That first evening had many sequels. Sometimes they joined some of Albert's friends, or the other cousins, other times they dined alone. Adela enjoyed each outing, but one evening asked her cousin, "When am I going to go to the opera?"

He replied, "When you are ready; you must study and listen to my records. That is the only way you will appreciate and really enjoy opera."

Albert had purchased the latest model of the phonograph that had been invented by Emile Berliner in1887. It played a flat disc instead of the cylinder Edison had invented for the recording of sound.

Adela was amazed at the record library her cousin had collected. He had every opera that had been recorded. So it was that she commenced her training for opera attendance. Albert started her on Carmen by Bizet. She had known certain parts and could hum "Habanera." But listening to the whole opera and following the libretto guaranteed that she would really appreciate the entire production. Five operas followed, first study and finally attendance at actual performances of Barber of Seville, La Boheme, Faust, Fledermaus, and Aida.

The German operas, The Ring, Tannhauser, Tristan and Isolde, he would leave for next season. Parsifal was being performed, but Albert said she was not ready for this music. She was disappointed, but thirty years later made up for it. She bought two tickets and a recording of the full opera. She and I played it several times. Finally we attended the "forbidden" Parsifal. "I don't know why Albert wouldn't let me see it; we understood and enjoyed it didn't we?" So there, Albert!

Opera was not the only activity planned for Adela. One was the trip to Buxtehude. When my mother said the word Buxtehude the word fascinated me as a child. It is such a euphonic word; one can say it over and over like a chant. But Buxtehude is an actual place. The family took their guest east of Kranz to the charming town. It had half—timbered style houses, St. Peter's church, a Gothic vaulted basilica built in 1296. But what delighted Adela was the regional museum, modeled after an old farm house. It reminded her of happy summers at her grandmother's house in Blankenese.

There were other outings my mother told me about. One the trip on her grandfather's ferry, and several evenings at a bier garten. The latter she did not enjoy. She could not drink the bitter, gas producing beverage, served in enormous tall steins. She would order lemonade, which could last a couple of hours with her ladylike sips. She could just sit there while her companions dashed off to relieve themselves—so vulgar, this eternal rushing off. The music and the jolly polka dancing she enjoyed, but not the beer drinking, and its result—No!

However, the long trip up the Elbe with her grandfather, now 78 years old, but spry as a thirty year old was a delight. They talked of the times she had spent with him in her girlhood. "You should have stayed in Germany, Adela. Your soul is German!"

All this had been wonderful, but all the while she kept remembering the boy with whom she went bicycling when she was in school here.

HERBERT

As my mother told me all about her second stay in Germany, my outstanding impression is that her romance with Herbert was the most important part, a deep emotional event that always stayed with her.

It started when she contacted Frau Kistler, the woman she had boarded with while in school. Frau Kistler was delighted to see her, and asked whether she had seen Herbert.

"No, I wouldn't know how to contact him, and besides it wouldn't be quite proper." Frau Kistler agreed, but came up with a solution. She would tell the gatekeeper, who was still employed by the Reits that Adela was back in Germany, visiting relatives. She would give him the phone number there, and was sure the gatekeeper would tell Herbert.

A week later, when luckily she was home, the maid came to her, "Frauline Suhr, there is a Herr Reit on the phone, wishes to speak to Frauline Suhr.

"Oh yes, I know him," Adela replied, and walked quickly to the telephone perched on the wall. "Yes, this is Adela. Oh yes, yes I remember you. I recall our going to visit your poor people, and of course the bicycle rides." A pause while she listened, clutching the long cylindrical earpiece jammed against her ear. "Yes, my cousin Albert, I am sure could take me from Kranz to Kiel to meet you. Next Tuesday? I will ask him. Phone me tomorrow and I shall have asked him if he is free." Albert was not free, but Fritz offered to take Adela. They were to meet at the Keinhaus Restaurant, this first time.

So commenced many more meetings in Kiel. There were seven more months of rendezvous, in late 1913 and early 1914. After that first time, Herbert always came to Kranz to pick her up in his elegant Daimler automobile.

The first two meetings they mainly talked of the past. Albert told Adela about his studies in land management. No matter how much land a family owned, they were not allowed to administer property, country or city, without a diploma in "Land Management." It would be at least another year before he could be on his own, controlling his own finances, establishing his own household.

But what of the romance? That they did fall in love I know for sure from my mother telling me. But details—did she ever meet his family? What did they talk about, plan? That my mother remained virginal, I am certain. She was such a deeply religious woman, strong in the Catholic belief in the importance of purity. But I do know that all the years she lived, she spoke of Herbert and his love. She well might have married him had it not been for two events; one immediate, the other several years later.

* * * * * * * *

WORLD WAR I

FIRST EVENT World War I broke out in April 1914. All foreigners had to leave immediately. Adela tried frantically to phone Herbert, but could not reach him. She had to leave without seeing or hearing from him.

SECOND EVENT Two years later, during the war, as a prisoner

in England, Herbert wrote a letter to Adela's address in Nicaragua. She had given it to him in case she had to return home in the months ahead. An aunt intercepted the letter and destroyed it. She didn't want her beloved niece going off back to Germany after the war. So it was that Adela finally believed Herbert had died.

Years later the aunt confessed; my mother was already married to my father and expecting her first child, me.

CHAPTER V -
LEAVES GERMANY/ USA VIA NICARAGUA

However, there were many events in Mama's life before she heard that confession.

When war broke out in August of 1914, all foreigners were ordered to leave the country. Before Adela fled to France, she had cabled the family in Nicaragua,

"LEAVING GERMANY. CONTACT ME AT NICARAGUAN EMBASSY IN PARIS. LOVE ADELA"

On the train trip across Germany into France she kept thinking of Herbert. Would she ever see him again; would he survive the war?

And her beloved relatives, what would happen to them? Finally, she thought of her father.

Aunt Sulema had written that he was not well. When Adela finally arrived at the Embassy in Paris, another letter awaited her. Her father was worse, "Come home as soon as possible."

She frantically tried to find a ship going directly to Central America. Nothing. She had to compromise for a passage to Florida, where she was to change to a small ship that would stop at Blue Fields, Nicaragua's eastern port. The weeks it took to finally arrive home to Managua were a torture of worry that she would not reach her father in time.

Her worst fears were realized when she finally arrived. My mother never got over the sorrow and guilt that she had not been at her dear papa's bedside. If she had only left Germany when she first heard he was ill.

The year of heavy black clothing, the weeping aunts and her young stepmother's confusion did not help Adelita overcome her sorrow. Not until a year later, when she went to the port of Corinto for a month, did she commence living a normal life. She had always loved the seaport town. Whenever my mother had her terrible bouts of Malaria, a stay in Corinto would heal her for the time.

Did my mother resume the round of parties and silly distractions when back in Managua? Partially yes, what else was there to do? However, having lived two years in well-ordered, prosperous Germany, the well to do young woman began to be concerned with the poverty surrounding her.

She heard of one sad case after another from servants. She felt herself very wise and worldly when she would insist on investigating in person a tale of someone in trouble—a sick child, a woman forced to flee a cruel husband but left without a penny to feed herself and the baby she had carried on her back wrapped in her shawl, a husband injured on a coffee plantation, but sent off by the heartless owner because he was not longer useful.

Every time she investigated in person, she found the actual conditions to be even worse than the facts the servant her given her. The actuality was always worse.

Her first investigation involved going to a little town that could be reached only by horseback or mule. Since childhood Adelita had ridden. She could even handle her father's Arabian. Besides being an accomplished horsewoman, the young lady was an excellent shot.

She seldom missed with either a rifle or a pistol. So she was not afraid of going to the mountains alone. She could take care of herself.

The woman who had been beaten by her husband was easy to help. Adelita simply had her brought to the house, warned the servants to keep her hidden. She added the woman, baby and all to her staff, with the stipulation that the girl was not to be sent on errands out of the house. Her husband would soon give up and find another woman.

Another story she investigated involved a man who had been hurt when he had fallen from a faulty ladder. He had badly injured his leg, and perhaps even his back. His fellow workers had complained in the past, asking the patron for a new ladder. "Do you think I am made of money?" he had yelled at them.

Now the men asked him for a loan of 2 mules that could hold a stretcher so the worker could be taken to a hospital. The patron not only refused, but fired the man. "He is no use to me now. Get him out of here."

Adelita found him in agony lying in a ramshackle hut, away from the plantation. She immediately found someone who would rent two mules. The workers had already prepared a primitive stretcher. Her next move was to hire four men who would transport the poor man to a hospital. She wrote a note for them to take to the hospital. It promised to pay whatever costs resulted in the worker being completely cured. Seniorita Suhr's credit was as good as cash.

Another case was the sick baby, no problem. She contacted her own doctor. She told him she was sending a mother with a sick baby to him. "Please see to it that this baby girl gets the best of care." Of course I will pay for a specialist if needed.

The doctor found that malnourishment was the problem. The mother's milk had almost dried up. She begged in the streets for money to buy milk, but it did not agree with her baby. So first the doctor gave the woman a formula that would agree with her child. Then he arranged with a convent, where he treated the nuns gratis, to take in the mother and child. She soon recovered her milk, and the child was completely cured..

A few days later her doctor came to see Adelita. In an uncle-like manner he told her, "Adelita, you must stop spending your money on these miserable poor. You are well off, but not a millionaire."

She agreed with him, but could not bear to say no when one more pitiful case came to her attention.

So into her private money she would go. How long would her inheritance from her mother's estate last? Adelita had relinquished the inheritance from her father in favor of her two little brothers, Albert and John. That way she hoped to have a voice in their upbringing. As I have said, their mother's idea of discipline was hitting the child on the head, especially Albertito. But it turned out there was nothing she could do to counteract the abuse suffered by her little brothers. She had given up her inheritance for nothing.

In the meantime, there was one person who had always been in the picture, in her life, her cousin Malcolm Arthur Nicol. In fact while she was still in Germany, Arthur had sent her a picture of himself, with the following note written on the back.

July 1914 To Adelita, the cousin I love most, Arthur And at the bottom he added; *"Although distance separates us, and my hand does not move to write often, Do not ever forget; never never, never forget that your cousin loves you.*

He began to visit more often, to tell her of his dreams of an export business. His few accounts had grown, and now new ones materialized when his reputation as an astute and honest businessman began to grow.

Adelita was proud of her cousin, and lately began to notice him looking at her in a different way. As he spoke of his future, he asked her opinion more and more and wanted suggestions from her. She felt something different in their relationship. Finally one day, Arthur proposed marriage. He said he had always loved her, but she seemed too remote. Now she seemed to be closer to him.

Adelita did not immediately give her cousin Arthur an answer; she waited a week, and deeply thought what life would be with this ambitious, honest man, so different from the men of total Nicaraguan ancestry. She compared him to Herbert, but that was no use, she was sure by now that Herbert was dead. So next time Arthur called, she said yes, she would marry him **HOWEVER**, she told him that she simply must leave this accursed country. Her Malaria attacks had become worse and more frequent. Unless she went to the coast and breathed in the ocean air she was down with one attack after another. T.B would be next! She had to get away from the tropics, near the ocean.

Her Uncle Alfredo Elizondo had moved to United States with his family when he was appointed Nicaraguan consul to San Francisco, the ocean air would cure her. Adela wanted to go to that city and become permanently established in the United States. After all, her father had become an American citizen.

"Arthur, you could run your business from there; an importer instead of an exporter. "Or,," she added, "One of the big companies would probably be glad to have you with your export experience, your total bilingual skills, "AND" she added with a giggle, "Your English gentleman handsome appearance."

"Marry me here, and I swear we will go to United States within a year."

"No, I cannot take a chance. Another year here I will be crazy, if I have not died from these awful bouts of Malaria, and this constant cough."

So it was settled. She would go to San Francisco and as soon as possible he would follow, and they would be married.

SAN FRANCISCO

Adela stood on the deck, all ready to disembark. Over her smart black suit, she wore a white fox boa, wrapped snugly around her throat against the wind and fog of San Francisco Bay. The weather was a huge change from the Nicaraguan tropics, but she loved it. And she loved the white city she saw as the ship progressed into the bay. When they finally docked, she tapped her high-heeled boot impatiently at the customs' delay.

But finally she was free and surrounded by her relatives, Uncle Alfredo and her cousins and their friends, who had come to welcome her. Oh, she could never never leave this wonderful city, this city where her new life was to begin.

Her uncle Alfredo Elizondo was Nicaraguan consul, and with his handsome sons and his two beautiful daughters, formed a social core of the Latin colony. There were Nicaraguens, Salvadoreans, Costa Ricans, as well as a sprinkling of wealthy South Americans. They had come to San Francisco for education, business, or simply to have a good time. Adelita's new life would begin with a round of parties to welcome the beautiful "Niña de los ojos tristes" (the girl with the sad eyes.) That is what these happy-go-lucky Latins were to call her.

When Uncle Alfredo, jaunty in his black Fedora, escorted her to the waiting Buick, he opened the door with the triangular Nicaraguen consular seal and said, "I've taken a lovely room for you right next door to the house we've leased in one of the best parts of San Francisco. Adelita was glad to hear she would be near them, and became more and more delighted with the fast paced city she observed as they proceeded through the narrow streets. San Francisco seemed to be one hill after another, with unbelievable views at the top.

When they passed a wide boulevard, Van Ness Avenue, her chattering cousins informed her they were entering the residential section, where soon they pulled up in front of a brown shingled house. As they climbed the wide stairs, the girls explained that this was a boarding house, established by an Irish widow, Mrs. Mary O'Connor. In addition to Adelita, there were four other guests. Mrs. O'Connor's three sons and two daughters completed the household.

The two daughters, Mary and Grace were in their twenties, like my mother, as were the boys, with the exception of Clifford, who was thirty. The family, especially the girls and Mrs. O'Connor remained friends all of my mother's life.

Mary and Grace both attended normal school when she arrived, but soon were established in the teaching profession. There they remained until retirement; neither married.

The two girls made her at home immediately, and weeks turned into months before she realized it. Mary and Grace were both attractive, with the redheaded, translucent skinned beauty of the Irish. They were as pure and proper as only devout, Irish Catholic girls could be, but my mother thought them a bit shocking. They went out alone with boys, and shaved their legs and armpits!

Adelita had an even more rigid idea of proper behavior for a young lady than had the Spanish girls she knew here and back in Nicaragua. Having had very little close adult supervision either in Nicaragua after her mother died or in Germany, my mother had to make her own rules. No one had complete authority over her, but she formed her own ideas of what was most respectable. Adelita never went to any social event without one or more of her male cousins escorting her. Besides, although six months had passed and Arthur still did not come, she considered herself engaged. His letters were full of love but also full of delays.

At first she didn't worry, took him at his word that business made it impossible to come. Maybe next month he would come and they could be married.

For a while she was too busy with parties and improving her English to notice the months passing by. Then the attentions of a serious, handsome young German-American, Mr. Schmidt kept her distracted. Still, she never went out alone with him, and always reminded the young man, if he seemed to be getting too serious, that she was engaged. He always was ready to take her cousins or a group of chattering girl friends in his Epperson automobile to wherever they want to go.

There were trips to the conservatory in to Golden Gate Park. Here Adelita's thoughts brought her back to Nicaragua, where she had created in her private patio, an authentic collection of tropical flowers. Another favorite outing was to the newly renovated Cliff House. They never could get enough of the vision of the turbulent Pacific Ocean.

Mr.Schmidt was very helpful with financial matters; Arthur had done all that for her in Nicaragua, after her father had died. Here in San Francisco, Schmidt seemed the only one stable enough to trust. She had questions about investing surplus money from her rentals in Nicaragua, or using that surplus to increase her real estate holdings in Nicaragua. He advised that trying to do real estate from a distance was too chancy. Better find income producing investments here in San Francisco.

Her male cousins were too full of their good times, the girls would know even less than she did, and her Uncle Alfredo always seemed too busy. Adela and Schmidt spoke a comic mixture of German and English, with a few Spanish words he knew thrown in.

About fourteen months after the end of World War I, Arthur was still tied down by his business in El Salvador. Adela began to wonder if perhaps she should accede to the pleadings in letters from her cousins in Germany. Albert and his parents wrote saying that although conditions in Germany were terrible—inflation, lack of work, the Feldmann family were prosperous because papa Feldmann had been able to make a good profit from the huge stock of premium wines he had collected for the Rathweinkeller. The only problem, Albert wrote, was "The horrible gang that has taken over the government." This was the beginning of the Hitler menace.

Adela and Mr. Schmidt discussed the possibilities of her making a trip to Germany. He was delighted at the thought of her going; it might break up that engagement of hers. So eagerly he exchanged dollars for Marks, and bought her passage to Germany. He even drove her to the telegraph office when she sent Arthur a cable, *"Tired of waiting, have booked passage for Germany. Will send address in Germany. Let me know when you are ready to come to San Francisco. Love Adelita."*

Two days later a messenger brought a cable from San Salvador for Adelita, "Taking next boat – cancel your trip. Love Arthur." It was followed a week later with another cable stating the ship and exact date of departure and arrival.

Sadly, Mr. Schmidt returned the tickets for her, re-exchanged the money, and instead helped her with errands in preparation for her wedding. Activity was frantic at her Uncle's house and even at Mrs. O'Connor's. When the sprightly lady saw her trying to find space in her room to make the bridesmaid's dresses, (her daughter Mary was one of the brides' maids) she patted my mother's hand and said, " Now, my dear, you can't possibly do all that in here. I have a little room with a window in the basement. You can have that for your sewing. I'm afraid you will be worn out on your big day."

Arthur arrived just two days before the wedding date, April 23, 1920, set by Adelita and her family and printed on invitations sent out to almost a hundred people, who filled the spacious Gothic St Dominic's church. Arthur was uncomfortable in this Catholic setting, and glad when they adjourned to the reception.

Mrs. O'Connor had offered the house, and had it decorated with garlands of flowers strung from plate rails. The April Wisteria was in full bloom, forming an archway at the entrance of the house. Adelita had arranged for catering, not wanting Mrs. O Connor to have further work. The floral decoration was enough.

When ever I see Wisteria I wonder if the young Nicol couple wondered what their life would be. What happiness, what sadness would be ahead.

CHAPTER VI
MARRIAGE—
CHILDREN, ARTHUR LEAVES

As they took off sorrow was the last thing on this young couple's mind. Arthur and Adelita rode in the chauffeured car loaned them by Arthur's English Uncle, John Nicol. "Uncle Jack" was a consulting engineer; he was pleased to offer his car and chauffeur to the young couple.

They stopped at fashionable Del Monte Lodge and toured Yosemite. Arthur and his new wife caught up on all the things they hadn't been able to say in letters. They discussed her dislike, no absolute loathing of people's pettiness, and the disparate distribution of wealth in Latin American countries. "Don't you really like North America better Arthur?

"Yes, if I can be in business for myself," He replied. They discussed his having to return to El Salvador because he had left unfinished business when he received Adelita's cablegram. But for now they just enjoyed each other and vowed to be separated as little as possible in the future. They would never let separations mar their marriage.

On their return, Mr.and Mrs.Arthur Nicol took a small apartment close to her uncle's house. Arthur would be leaving as soon as he had his new wife established. He laughed at her attempts to cook. Mrs. O'Connor would never let anyone in her kitchen, and her uncle's house had been too hectic.

The new Mrs. Nicol's first attempt in the kitchen was applesauce. She filled a huge pot with water and dumped in the peeled and cored apples—that is what the cookbook said to do. Adelita checked the pot a couple of hours later, and found nothing. The apples had disintegrated with so much water. The book had not said exactly how much water nor how many apples were needed, so she thought the more water the better. Then when Adelita would burn something in her confusion of trying to cook two things at once. Arthur would laugh and they would trot off and have dinner out. It was a long time before Adelita could put together an entire dinner. How she regretted not having taken advantage of the chance to have cooking lessons in Germany! Her uncle's chef at the Rathweinkeller had offered to teach her the art of cuisine.

"I'll never have to cook," Adela told him. "I would never marry a man who couldn't afford servants."

After two months when Arthur tried doing business by mail and telegraph, it became evident that he must return to Salvador to complete the business he had left so precipitously when Adelita had threatened him with a trip to Germany. She hated to see him go, and furthermore began to suspect she might be pregnant. Adelita knew that a total change of life, like losing virginity, all the excitement of the wedding and the honeymoon, of trying to be an American housewife, all this could affect a woman's menstrual cycle; but three months had passed without a period. Arthur insisted his wife see a doctor, but before they could get an appointment he had to leave.

So it was that by letter Adelita gave him the news; how she wished she could have seen his face when he learned he was to be a father.

During the three months he was gone, Adelita was so busy that she found it difficult to write the biweekly letters he seemed to expect. Had she had experience in the details of keeping house, cooking, food shopping, cleaning, laundry there would have been plenty of time to write even daily letters. But as she had bumbled the applesauce, she continued to be overwhelmed by tasks that were simple to American housewives.

The little apartment they had first taken proved uncomfortable; it was cold and had only one bathroom. Arthur made a ritual of toilet time because since childhood constipation had cursed him. He needed a long time and liked having his own bathroom.

Another reason to move was that a servant girl, Rosa, who as a mere child had been a maid in Adelita's house in Nicaragua, had written hoping to come to San Francisco. Could she come to Niña Adelita's home?

Poor families put their daughters out to serve when they reach 14 years of age, some even as young as 12. They are sent to a "good" family at pennies per week until they have learned housework. Then they can hire out at $5.00 a month! Rosa had been such a child.

The young girl had been working as a regular maid for three years, but knew she would remain a servant with hand to mouth wages all her life. If Rosa had a place to stay in the United States, she could find a maid's job that would pay her enough to save money, and maybe someday buy a little store in Nicaragua and be on her own. So she had written Niña Adelita, whom she knew was kind and would help her.

Adelita remembered Rosa as bossy, willing and very bright—as bright, she considered, as an Indian could be. In those days my mother was still infected with the white supremacy that is as bad in Latin America as it is in our Southern States. Later my mother softened, but she was never completely cured of prejudice.

Rosa's letter had come at a good time. Adelita found a spacious apartment that they could afford; it had two and a half bedrooms, and most important two bathrooms! The half bedroom was really a large closet, with a glass door to a small yard. It would be fine for Rosa's bedroom. She would write Rosa, "Yes, come." My mother had dreaded moving all by herself. There would be a month before she had to change residence.

Rosa immediately bought her passage, and was to arrive before moving time. On the date the ship docked Adelita took the dinky—that is what locals called the San Francisco Cable car—to the waterfront. She boarded the ship, found the frightened girl, and helped her get through customs and immigration. Rosa was allowed to come as a permanent resident because Mrs. Arthur Nicol had vouched the girl would not become a burden on the community. In fact, she came as an actual employee of the Nicols.

Rosa carried her one little suitcase to the cable car; it was walking distance from the piers. They boarded the Sacramento Street Car, which went through Chinatown. Adelita thought the girl from Nicaragua would be excited to see all the "Chinos." Instead poor Rosa was terrified when she heard a terrible sound of bangs and whistles; she clung to her patron. It was Chinese New Year, which she had never heard of; she thought it was a revolution.

Adelita explained that these were firecrackers, and that in United States there were no revolutions as in Nicaragua. The girl was relieved, but glad when they passed that horrible district with all those strange Chinese people.

By the time Arthur returned in December of 1920, the new apartment was in order. Rosa was still with her; the girl had not had the nerve to go looking for work. She would accept no wage, though she took care of all the housework and cooking.

So there was plenty of time for Arthur and Adelita to talk. They called each other by a Spanish baby talk version of "amor". It became "Moy" for him, and "Moycia" for her.

There was plenty to talk about; Arthur was full of enthusiasm about a new venture he was starting. "Darling, you have done very well, but soon you will have a cook and a maid; maybe you would like to keep Rosa, she seems very good. Soon you'll only go in the kitchen when you feel like it." He went on to tell her about the man he had met on the ship coming home; he had the rights to a wonderful patent medicine that he wanted to market. Arthur painted such a promising future for the medicine, that Adelita almost caught his enthusiasm. When he said that there would have to be capital to launch the enterprise, they discussed Adelita's selling one of her houses in Nicaragua. He and the owner of the patent would form a company. Arthur's partner would run the business, and Arthur would continue with his Central American business until the partnership was bringing in enough to support them both.

But, Moy," Adelita said, as they sat cozily on the sofa, "Maybe you should think instead of joining a big export import firm. They would pay wages— you are so smart and experienced they soon would make you a manager. A firm like Otis McAllister would love to have you."

Arthur sat up stiffly, looked at his wife and replied, "If you have such faith in me, you would support me in this patent medicine business that I want to start. I don't want just a salary. I want to be rich, not have to kowtow to some stupid owner, just because he inherited the business. I am just as good as they are. What's the matter? Don't you want to lend me your money?"

"Of course, of course, darling," and she put her fingers on his cheek. "What's mine is yours, there is no lending and paying back in a marriage. I'll write my lawyer right away and tell him to sell the Calle Francisco house. Meantime he can take out a loan on it, so that you can have the money immediately." Arthur snuggled contentedly against her, "Yes Moycia, that is a capital idea."

By the time they had completed the many details involved in starting a business, including obtaining the capital from Nicaragua, it was time to prepare for the first Christmas together.

Adelita was very large by now, and only when Arthur would

walk with her at night would she go out of the house. The doctor had insisted Adelita must walk. Exercise was important for an easier delivery. But she was ashamed to be seen in the daytime, and would only go out walking at night if Arthur accompanied her. But often he had night meetings with his partner and could not take his wife for a walk. Mama told me "I paid the price of that neglect in a difficult delivery of my little Mary."

Arthur would return from the sessions with his partner with a glum look, and finally spilled out, things were not going well. But he was still hopeful, really believed in the product they were trying to launch. He was most grateful when Adelita gave him the rents that had been collected for her remaining properties in Nicaragua.

On February 12th, 1921, Lincoln's birthday, Mary Adele was born at the Saint Francis hospital, just two blocks from their apartment. Those were the days when a mother stayed two weeks in the hospital. There was enough money to pay that, but Dr. Reginal Smith had to wait for part of his fee.

Adelita had lost hope in the new business. Money was just not coming in but plenty was going out. With a baby to care for now, she wanted more security and begged Arthur to drop it all and find a paying job. She didn't care if he ever replaced the money that had gone into the business.

"Just let's not get into more debt," she implored. But Arthur was adamant. "Believe in me darling, I will make a go of it. " But more debts kept mounting up. Rosa was still with them. She asked for no salary, and still did not look for work; she couldn't leave Niña

Adelita with the baby. Rosa knew of the financial situation and agreed that Don Arturo should get a regular job. For six months the two women discussed what might be done. "Maybe you should get a job sewing at one of those fancy dress designers. A friend of mine works for a Madame Nicolini. I can take care of the baby, and have dinner ready for you."

So it was that Adelita finally took matters into her own hands. A week after the conversation with Rosa, Adelita came home one late afternoon after a trip downtown. Arthur was already home and was amazed to see her exquisitely dressed in one of her trousseau suits. She sat down, before even taking off her hat and gloves, "Arthur, I have taken a job sewing for a fashionable couturier, Madame Nicolini."

At first Arthur couldn't believe it, his princess, the girl who had never done anything but spend money, who still couldn't cook very well, earning money!

"Moycia, are you strong enough? You don't have to you know; I'll manage somehow."

But she assured him, "No, I am sure I can do it. Madame Nicolini said she would teach me. When I took my suit coat off and showed her the blouse I was wearing, that I had made, she seemed impressed. I start next Monday."

Adelita did well at Madame Nicolini but had no intentions of commencing a career. She merely wanted Arthur to realize that he must must get a regular job. He finally did inquire at an export import firm, Hamburger Polhemus . Mr. Polhemus was delighted to learn of Arthur's experience. He introduced him to the other members of the small company; Mr. Hamburger, his partner, an elderly gentleman soon to be retired; Mr. Sherry, the accountant, a stylish young fellow, his hair parted in the middle, the "in" thing during the twenties 20's and Mrs. Rabe, his secretary, a tall, prematurely white haired woman. With the office boy, a couple of clerks, the staff was complete. Arthur could see how they all added affection to the respect they had for their "boss."

Polhemus would like Arthur to be his traveling man. He was tired of the constant trips to Central and South America. The firm had much business in Peru and Columbia; did Mr. Nicol know that territory?

"No, my business has been all in Central America, but I am certain I would quickly learn the ropes in South America; as long as it isn't Brazil, it would take me a while to learn Portuguese." Polhemus admired the young man's self assurance and putting out his hand said, "We would certainly like to have you aboard Nicol. What do you say?"

After they had discussed salary and expense account arrangements, chances for advancement, Arthur signed the needed papers and left his smiling employer to give his Adelita the news.

She arrived home after he did. When he saw her tired face, he was glad he had finally given up and taken a job. Later, he would consider going into business for himself. The patent medicine business would have succeeded if he had had a decent partner. He even slightly suspected that the man had not been entirely honest with him. But that was all over now. He hurried to make his wife comfortable and tell her all about his new job.

"Darling, all our troubles are over, you can stop working. My poor Moicia looks so tired. Come get your feet up, I'll get you a refresco." They chattered on all evening, and only regretted that traveling would be required again, but glad that they would be able to pay the debts and start living again.

The next day Adelita gave her notice to a very upset Madame Nicolini. "You were learning so much; I thought maybe someday you could become an associate. You are such a lady, you could deal with my clients. Go now, Adela, but think it over, you could go places in the fashion world."

As my mother continued telling me of the early years of their marriage she told me," I told Madame that I would think about it but there it stopped. I knew my smart handsome husband was going to be a great success. I would have my hands full being a good wife, a hostess, and of course a good mother."

A week after Adelita was home again, Rosa announced that now she did feel confident to seek the job for which she had come to United States. Niña Adelita didn't need her any more. She promised she would come often to see her "chichi", as she always called me. She adored "la chichi" and loved getting the little girl dressed up and taking her to meet the many friends she had made when taking the baby out to the park.

It seemed half of Nicaraguen servants had spilled out of that country and were in San Francisco, holding down good paying jobs as nursemaids and upstairs or downstairs maids. The men were chauffeurs or gardeners.

I was one when Rosa left, but she kept her promise and often came to take me to see her friends. She insisted I be all dressed up, and if my mother hadn't had time to iron one of my many frilly little dresses, Rosa would pull out the ironing board and quickly prepare what she considered proper garb for "her" baby.

After Rosa left, my father had to go on a long trip for the firm. There were still debts to pay off, and furthermore, Adelita was lonesome, and a little frightened in that large apartment. So she put an ad in the paper to rent one of the bedrooms. She was apprehensive about having a stranger in the house, but the loneliness and the money to be made gave her courage.

The lady who answered the ad and rented the room made Adelita's fears seem foolish. Mrs. Kennedy was a middle-aged sales lady at Davis Schmoeser. Typical of sales ladies at exclusive stores, she had a gentle refinement. Later, she proved to be a real friend.

I had frequent bouts of Bronchitis and cried a great deal at night. My mother would get me up for fear of disturbing the neighbors and her new tenant. One night I had a high fever and my mother was frantically trying to lower it with cold towels and rubbing alcohol. Mrs. Kennedy got up and helped in spite of my mother's protestations that her tenant needed her sleep. But, dear soul that she was, Mrs. Kennedy repeated her kind act many times before my father returned from his trip of thirteen months.

He did not like it a bit that there was a stranger in the house, so diplomatically his wife had to tell Mrs. Kennedy that she would have to find another room. Considerate person that she was, Mrs. Kennedy understood, and told Adelita, "Your husband must come first, my dear. I only wish I had my dear husband; he died five years ago. Appreciate your husband while you have him."

Now my parents were alone in that spacious apartment. But it was not spacious enough that Daddy wouldn't hear me cry. I am told that when I started to cry at night, he would simply go "grrr" in his big deep voice, and immediately I would hush up. So maybe Mary had become rather spoiled by the two ladies.

My father had done so well on his long trip to South America, that Mr. Polhemus made him general manager. Arthur had recovered a debt that no one had been able to collect. His combination of English coolness and tenacity together with Spanish charm and knowledge of Latin American ways had won. Where a smart American, Mr. Polhemus, with an adequate knowledge of Spanish had been unable to succeed, my father, with the background of Latin American subtleties was able to pull it off. He was raised to $500 a month, a sizeable salary in 1922.

It was a comfortable income, however, because a new baby was on the way, due in March of 1923, my mother felt she needed a little extra. She wanted to hire a nurse to care for her and the new baby. When Mary had been born, she did have Rosa to help; but seeing the girl had no salary, Adelita had tried to do as much of the work as possible.

One afternoon she went up to the clotheslines on the roof of the apartment house, to hang some wet diapers. My mother caught a terrible cold in her breasts. So she was determined that with this new baby she would have adequate help.

So it was she wrote her lawyer in Nicaragua and told him to sell her last house. As luck would have it, one of Adelita's uncles needed a house for his three sisters. He bought Adelita's house, installed the elderly ladies. They now had a secure place to live for the rest of their gentle, protected lives.

My mother was able to have her second child, Malcolm in peace, without worry about from where the doctor's fee was coming. Furthermore, she was able to have a nurse at home to tend her and the baby, and there was plenty of money left over. Adelita intended investing it in property right here in her beloved San Francisco.

The location she best liked was the Marina, adjacent to the site of the 1918 World's Fair. Adelita would have liked a lot right on Marina Boulevard, overlooking the bay and the proposed Yacht Harbor. But this property was too expensive. Then she was shown a lot directly across the Palace of Fine Arts, with its lake made picturesque by swans and ducks. It was the only building left standing after the fair.

She and Arthur took a streetcar down to see it, and he thought the site perfect. He could picture their house, with lots of room for help, and a separate yard for the children. He put his arm around his wife, "Oh how I longed for a house of our own, Moycia." She quietly answered, "Yes, it will be so good." At this point there was no more conversation about building a house right away.

So Adelita contacted the agent, wrote a check for the entire cost of the lot. When she had the deed, she gave it to Arthur saying, "Put this in our safe deposit box. It will be safe until we need it."

"What for?" he replied. "We'll need the deed as soon as we find a builder and know what kind of loan we will need."

"But Darling, I don't want to build now. It's too isolated down there. I want to wait until Malcolm can walk, until more people have built there. I would be petrified living alone when you are on your trips."

"But I want a house now; we live like rats, so crowded, people next to us, on top of us. When we have a servant, I don't like her right on top of us."

With variations this conversation was repeated over and over during the ensuing weeks. Each time the pitch of their voices grew higher. "I want to have a house now, now!"

"I'm afraid to live in such an isolated area. After all my money bought that lot." Gone was her "What's mine is thine" attitude.

Finally he went out looking for houses. Sometimes he would take me with him. I was a cheerful little thing and adored my daddy.

One rainy day he took me for a long walk. I was all galloshed, rain- coated, and muffled, delighted at this adventure Daddy and I were having. Daddy had made a date with a real estate man to see a little Victorian on Baker Street. The agent was waiting in front of the house. My father and the man went over the entire house, basement, tiny apartment upstairs, kitchen and spacious yard. "The little apartment would make a good study for me," remarked daddy. Then he turned to me," Do you like it Mary Adele?"

"Oh yes" What did I know of houses, but my Daddy liked it, must be wonderful.

My father and the real estate man went into earnest conversation. I only got words; Lot Marina—Sell—Down payment—consult wife; and a lot of other words I couldn't understand. When we returned home I thought mama would be happy about the house. Instead, my parents started shouting. Papa ended by slamming out of the house, and mama by crying and crying.

When Daddy returned, he wouldn't talk to her-nor the next day, nor the next. His silent treatment went on for two weeks. Finally my mother gave up and said she would sell the lot, and they would buy the house on Baker Street. She had gone to see it, and didn't like it much. It seemed damp, but the real estate man assured her that when the furnace was lit, it would warm up.

So we moved to the Baker Street house. I have good memories of that house, of a wonderful little room in the basement, of seeing more of my Daddy than I ever had; I guess he was making fewer trips at this time. I also remember the Irish girl, Brady; my mother had hired her to care for my little brother Malcolm. I don't remember liking her, I can see her pinched little face and straight blond hair. But I am told she was utterly devoted to the "baiby."

That's all I remember about Baker Street. But my mother later told me that the house was damp, that the furnace never worked well, that a new roof had to be put on. She said I was getting paler and thinner and had a constant cough.

My parents' fights grew more frequent. I believe they were mostly about my declining health. The mother tiger was not going to let her cub die. So finally my parents leased the house and moved to a small apartment on Jackson Street. It had only one bedroom, one bath. I believe it was chosen because it was near the school where I was to start kindergarten.

Brady, the Irish nursemaid was put in the dinette, but didn't last long. She announced, "I don't likes to sleep in the kitchen." So now there was no help. It was near summer when Brady left and it did seem foolish to get another girl in that small place. My father was going on another trip to South America for his company, so they decided that they would take the children to the country for the summer.

My mother hated the country, "It's so uncivilized," but perhaps because of her happy times in the countryside of Germany she felt it was good for us. The summer rental column in the Chronicle yielded a promising ad.

FAMILY ACCOMODATIONS; ROOM AND BOARD. GOOD GERMAN COOKING.

My mother phoned the Mill Valley number and made an appointment for the next week; Meanwhile she helped Daddy pack for his next business trip.

We made the first of many San Francisco bay crossings by ferry to Sausalito, where we boarded the electric train to Mill Valley. It sped along a tree-lined track. When we arrived, we took a jitney driven by a fat jolly man named Ray.

Mr. Shuler was waiting for us at the bottom of a steep hill, crisscrossed with paths between a rich variety of bushes and flowers. "Ahch, keeping this hill from sliding away makes always the work." I had never heard a German accent and was fascinated. Both of us instantly liked the tall, slightly balding man, but my brother and Mr. Schuler formed a relationship much needed by my brother with his ever absent father.

Mr.Schuler taught Malcolm to hammer his first nail, always defended him when my active brother got into trouble; the little boy supplied a void that his two daughters, Frida and Elsie, much as he loved them, couldn't fill.

When we finally reached the top, there was mama Schuler, wrapped in a large white apron, her blond hair with streaks of white, rolled into a knot top her round head. Her sensibly shod feet were planted on the beautifully polished front door stoop.

"Come in, come in and have some coffee." She almost shooed us in, afraid the flies might come into her impeccable house. "Come in, come in and have some coffee." She served a wonderful buttery coffeecake, with milk for us and coffee for the grownups. We sat in a sunny little breakfast room, papered in a bright orange floral pattern.

When we had finished, Mrs. Schuler ushered us into a little guest bathroom where she instructed us to wash our "schmery" hands. Then the Schulers and the Nicol family went downstairs to the lower floor. Here there was the rumpus room, with a small bedroom adjoining. The full length porch outside the large room gave the quarters a complete apartment feeling.

"It's perfect! When can we move in? We would like to spend the summer months here."

"Any time." Said Mr. Schuler.

"Any time" turned into two weeks. My mother cleared all our closets; put an ad offering the Jackson Street apartment as a summer rental She accepted a couple from New York. They were in San Francisco for the summer. Finally by June we were all packed up into a friend's car and on our way to Mill Valley.

I told Mama once that I understood why she loved Germany and German people so much. I said to her "That summer, and the next two, that we spent at the Schuler's were some of the happiest of my life." Their home centered way of life, and their German competence in all phases of homemaking, from cooking to cleaning, gardening, carpentry, home canning, had a profound influence on me.

The Schuler's house was the center of their lives, with the kitchen its heart. Here bread was baked on Saturdays for the week; mayonnaise was made from scratch—my mother didn't even use mayonnaise, let alone make it. She felt food was meant to keep the body alive;" the less time spent on its preparation the better.

What was important was to spend time with her two little children. She told us stories, took us on long walks to Uncle Jack's, about two miles from the Schuler's. I remember her laughing and joking; she was such a happy mamita then.

As we sat properly in the living room, one late afternoon, Mrs. Schuler confided to my mother that when we had first come to see the house, she had been surprised at how young we were; she had been hesitant about taking us. But now she saw we were really such good "kinder," because we had been strictly brought up—not like these Americans. The good lady considered my mother German, because she frequently conversed with the Schulers in their native language. She was still totally fluent in German.

In late August my father returned. The San Francisco apartment had been sublet until October, so he came to the Schuler's. He enjoyed the wonderful food, Charleston dancing with the two Schuler girls and their high school friends in the evening. Besides the frivolity, Arthur loved his long talks with Mr. Schuler, who had a good education, and a broad background. He was an executive with Hercules Powder Company, and had amassed a marvelous collection of guns. Only because building their house had cost more than they had planned, did the Schulers resort to taking summer guests.

Several times, my father brought business clients to the house for an even more sumptuous meal than usual. There was wine, and often Mr. Schuler's potent home brewed beer. Prohibition was in force, but I guess the grownups had the right connections.

We children, of course, were kept in the background, but I knew when I grew up I would have wonderful parties like that! My parents seemed so happy there, what a shame they had to go back to the cramped little apartment on Washington Street. Just a few incidents and impressions mark that winter in my memory.

* * * * * * * * * * * * *

The single bathroom was cause of much conflict, especially the time I had Ptomaine poisoning. Because he had always had a problem with constipation, my father always spent hours in the bathroom. That morning my mother wildly knocked on the door, screaming, "Mary is sick, she has to throw up!"

I don't remember whether I ever got the bathroom. But I can't ever forget the terrible gash on my Daddy's cheek! My mother dug her nails into him in her fury that her baby had not immediately been given access to the sacred bathroom.

I also remember that at Christmas time, the tree was put in the hall. We had to be very quiet for a long time until our Daddy woke up. I remember being shushed a great deal when he was asleep or working at his desk in the living room. As a contrast to the scratch on the cheek, let me say my mother did try to manage, keeping his sense of being "El Senior" in those cramped quarters. But I guess the tension would erupt, living in those two rooms with only one bath must have been a strain.

My mother slept in the bedroom with us, and my father on the wall bed in the living room. He used this same room as an office. Besides keeping up his increasingly heavy load at Hamburger Polhemus, he was studying Auto Mechanics at night. He was planning a trip to Guatemala to help his brothers with their Chrysler agency. He felt he needed to know cars from the inside out.

This was a period when I remember my father stern, always working, and a bit frightening. My mother was always shushing us, not just Christmas morning. Only once I remember him happy, and playing with us.

This was around Christmas time; my mother had invited Uncle Jack, his wife aunt Tousie, and her sisters, delicate, giggly old maid retired school teacher Aunt Bruce, and stern, straight rigid Christian Scientist, Aunt Georgie.

I guess my father got a little bored, and accepted when a neighbor asked him in for a drink or two or three. Anyway, when he came back to his own apartment, he ended up sitting on the floor with us, playing with our toys. The stiffer and more disapproving the aunties became, the more he laughed, and finally, "This party is too dull; I think I'll go back upstairs, they are a much jollier bunch." He didn't, of course, but years later my mother would giggle at remembering how shocked the proper English relatives had been. She remarked, half in jest, "Your father should have gotten tipsy more often; he would have been better off." My father was so unswerving in his drive toward a goal, poor Arthur.

* * * * * * * * * *

Finally his Auto Mechanics course was completed; several pieces of business he was to do for his firm were arranged, and Daddy was off again; this time to Guatemala. He was to be there until the next summer, when he would join us again in Mill Valley.

As I think back on my parents I better understand. My mother too, was unswerving, but her ways were subtle. I see the pattern of their doomed marriage now; both of them in classic tragedy mode; going from event to event to the inevitable conclusion.

Their religious attitudes were fundamental to their conflicts. Both Adelita and Arthur had Catholic mothers. The family lived in a then exclusively Catholic country, Nicaragua. They were baptized in the Catholic Church. My German grandfather could care less, and my English grandfather had no Episcopal clergy to back him up, if he had cared about having his children baptized in that faith.

However, as soon as his children, Celia, Charley, Henry, Arthur and even little seven year old Dick were old enough, they were shipped off to England to a "good" Protestant school. Only baby Maria remained at home. Here my father learned about the Papist's evil ways, and was properly confirmed in the Church of England.

My mother, as I have said, received her education in Germany. She always considered herself a Catholic. She had had a deep religious experience during her first Communion at the Assumption Convent. Although she was only allowed to stay one year, the Catholic training became deeply ingrained. It was tested when she was sent to school in Northern Germany. There were simply no facilities for Catholic instruction; not even a Catholic church. German law stated that all children must receive religious instruction. My mother remembers all the Jewish children going off to Jewish religion classes, but for her, the only solution the law abiding Germans could find was to insist she attend the Lutheran classes right there in her school.

The twelve-year-old Adela gave "those Protestants" passive resistance. During the class she would take the bread out of her lunch box and make little statues, putting all her concentration on her task lest the "wrong" things they were saying should get into her mind. Years later when she lived with the staunchly Irish Catholic O'Connors, her anti Protestant prejudice was reinforced.

So how did these two, Arthur and Adelita fall in love and marry? Somehow my mother maneuvered her fiancée to consent to being married as a Catholic because he had been baptized in that faith. I suppose Arthur considered it a matter of form, not really a denial of his Protestantism; he even went through the motions of Confession.

But immediately after the honeymoon, he went to his church and she went to hers. He would always tell her he had an open mind, and she made a vague attempt to find, a broad minded priest who would not infuriate him; but she was unsuccessful.

On Sundays the four of us would take the California street cable car to church. He always got off at Grace Cathedral and we went on to Old St. Mary's.

A few times he said to my brother, "Wouldn't you like to go to

Daddy's church?" But my mother was too quick, she would whisper in the little boy's ear, "Don't you dare, I'll spank you if you go." And of course Malcolm would say, no he wanted to go with mama.

Another point of religious disagreement was birth control. The Catholic Church forbids it. My mother would have no part of the practice. However, my father had no such reservations. He had decided that for now two children were enough.

He would tease my mother, saying, "You don't really want any more children, but are secure in putting the blame for prevention on me." She would violently protest and wish she could prove that she was sincere. She had her chance when he came back from a long trip to South America. It was summer, so the family was again installed in Mill Valley at the Schuler's, with all the surrounding beauty and relaxing atmosphere.

As Adelita unpacked his bags, she realized that he did not have his birth control equipment. The stores were miles away, and by the time she and Arthur would retire for the night, it would be too late to buy anything. She encouraged him to have plenty of Mr. Schuler's delicious beer, and when at last they left the others, she was ready to prove she could be a loving wife without birth control.

Two and a half months later she was sure her faith had been confirmed when she saw her doctor, who said yes, she was pregnant. Arthur was not too pleased, but was kind when even in her seventh month she felt miserable. To make matters worse, an emergency came up and the company needed Arthur to make a trip to Peru. My mother begged him not to go, but he insisted it was absolutely necessary.

"You can call Mrs. Schuler; I am sure she could use a little extra money to care for the children when you go to the hospital. And who knows, I may be able to return in time for the baby's birth."

No matter how she pleaded, became angry, cried, he would not change his plans. She had such a deep feeling of something going wrong. It was the first of two premonitions of tragedy that were proven true. The second would concern my brother Malcolm, eighteen years later.

Mrs. Schuler did come to take care of us when my mother's time came. I remember Mama leaving the house crying, her face very red. In those days children were not told about babies; we were told simply that maybe mama would come back with a little brother or sister.

When the baby was born, Mrs. Schuler took us to the hospital to see mama and our new little brother Maurice Albert. Malcolm and I were thrilled to see the tiny little red thing shown to us through a glass pane in the nursery.

Apparently when it was time to feed him, he would be asleep and refuse to wake and take nourishment. When later he was awake and crying for food, it was not feeding time and nurses refused to give him nourishment. My mother was very sick and didn't realize what was happening. By the time the doctor was called, the poor baby was totally dehydrated. Maurice Albert was born July 4th 1927, but by July 7th we no longer had a little brother!

It sounds unbelievable, but this is the story my mother told me. I was terribly sorry mama was so sad and upset, but was rather excited at the thought that we had our own private little angel in heaven, I thought dead babies became angels.

It was a moral blow to my mother. This pregnancy had been her proof to God that she believed all the teachings of the Catholic Church, including the prohibition against birth control. Was this how God repaid her faith? Why had He done this?

My mother was so ill that she had to stay two weeks in the hospital, and then only if she brought a nurse home with her would they release her. My mother never again regained the vigor she had on our long walks in Mill Valley. I don't remember her laughing much after Maurice Albert died.

We did go to Mill Valley to the Schuler's when mama was stronger, and again my father returned and came there after his South American trip. I asked him if he was sad about the baby dying, and he said yes; later my mother said he was relieved. He denied that, so I don't know.

From Mill Valley I started school. My mother had enrolled me at the Convent of the Sacred Heart before the baby was born. So when the glorious day came I walked down the hill with my daddy, wearing my brand new black serge uniform, with stiffly starched collar and cuffs. We boarded the train, then the ferry, and finally the number 3 streetcar, which went directly to the school on Jackson Street. For a whole month Daddy and I made the wonderful trip to San Francisco and then back to Mill Valley in the late afternoon. After that month the family returned to San Francisco to the Jackson Street apartment

When Daddy was home, not on a trip, he took a great interest in what I was learning at school. Before I went to bed, he would come in the bedroom and coach me in French; he must have learned it at his English school. Then there was my defense of religion. He would ask me questions. Lord knows how or what I answered. He did not believe in praying to saints as Catholics do. He asked me once, "If I were dead, would you pray to me?"

"Oh no, Daddy" I replied, "Because you are not a saint." My innocent reply made Daddy laugh.

But he didn't laugh about the little cat. My mother to the end of her days loathed cats, with almost paranoia. There were always cats walking on the back fence. She would shudder and say, "Ugh, filthy creatures."

One day Arthur brought home a little stray kitten. We loved it, but I guess Adelita made his life so impossible that he finally took it off some place. *"No me permiten tener el gatito,"* (They wont let me have the little cat.) He told us sadly.

But Adelita and Arthur were in total agreement when it came to plans for the future. One day my mother sat us down for a serious talk.

"Your Daddy is not going to work for Mr. Polhemus any more. He is going to Guatemala and will be in business for himself. He will help his brothers with the Chrysler agency, but mainly work on his own accounts." To be assured of an immediate income, he had contracted with Hamburger Polhemus to represent the company in Central America. Rather than receive commission, he was to have a retainer, a check that was to be sent directly to Mrs. Nicol for the household expenses. The arrangement was to last until Arthur became established in Guatemala. He was sure he would be rich in five years. Meanwhile he planned to come home every Christmas, with the exception of the current year.

Although they were sad at parting, my parents were sure their lives were changing for the better—times were booming. He had been such a success with Polhemus, on his own he would do magnificently. It was June 4, 1929, the day after his 35th birthday, which had been forgotten in the rush of getting him ready for the trip. My mother felt terrible, and kept apologizing to him and saying to us, "Isn't it terrible, your poor Daddy, we forgot his birthday." He just looked sad, birthdays were important in our family.

We all boarded the huge ship and eagerly inspected Daddy's stateroom. Malcolm and I thought it was so cute, just a bed and bureau and a funny little round window way up high. He unlatched it for us and carefully taught us the correct word for this little window. "Porthole, porthole." We repeated, giggling each time, such a funny word.

But Malcolm was nervous and wanted to leave. "Wouldn't you like to go with your papi?"

Malcolm didn't understand—if it meant leaving mama—no!

The five year old boy said nothing, and my father turned to Adelita, hurt in his golden brown eyes. But then the ship's horns blasted and a steward paraded the decks, "All ashore that's going ashore, all visitors ashore."

One last hug and kiss and we carefully went down the gangplank. The three of us stood on the dock waving and waving and crying until the tug pushed the ship away from us, around the corner, until it disappeared behind the northern piers. We could imagine the big boat going out the Golden Gate, so Daddy was gone. This seemed different from his other trips.

CHAPTER VII
LIFE DURING DEPRESSION
1929 – 1930

Once home the three of us eagerly awaited my father's letters. Meanwhile mama made plans for the rest of summer. She began to worry about both Malcolm's and my health. We did not seem to recover from the tonsil operation we had two months ago. Both of us were pale and listless.

Mama complained to her friend, Matilde "It is so cold here, I wish I could take the children south to warm weather" Her friend replied, "Don't you know someone in Southern California who could find you something near the beach?"

"Yes, my friends the Throsbys could probably help. Good idea .Matilde!"

When mama wrote Muriel Throsby asking her to inquire about

a rental by the ocean. Three letters and a phone call finally resulted in a move to a wonderful little cottage right on the beach in Santa Monica.

All in a week my mother had put our furniture in storage, given up the Jackson Street apartment and transported the three of us by train to Los Angeles. Ray and Muriel Throsby picked us up at the train station, drove us to Santa Monica, right to the cottage, that they had rented for the Nicol family.

Malcolm and I lived in our bathing suits, running in and out of the house. Sand didn't matter; there were no rugs, so sand could just be swept out. We thought mama was so clever; she could make cottage cheese out of the milk that was eternally going sour. Neither refrigerator nor icebox had been supplied.

Next mama put a little ocean water in a glass and set it in the sun for a week. We kept going to peek, and then, "Oh mama you are so smart, there is salt at the bottom of this glass you filled with sea water."

Muriel Throsby had to go east to visit her mother, but Ray came frequently to visit us. He always wore crisp white trousers, and his white shoes seemed huge to us children. A couple of times Ray took the three of us to Venice, the adjoining town, where he treated us to the milder amusement rides. I liked the bump cars. It seemed so wicked to crash into another car on purpose!

All three months we were in Santa Monica, Daddy and Mama corresponded weekly. In letter after letter Mama kept insisting that the Baker Street house should be sold because it was so difficult to keep rented and furthermore, *"I just couldn't live there again because of the dampness."*

Daddy wrote; *"Moycia dear; I guess you win, go ahead and sell the Baker Street house. Some day we will buy a house that you like."* He continued the letter with discouraging news about business.

On our return to San Francisco we moved to Baker Street, but only till it could be sold. Mama put us into the little apartment she had built in the attic and left the main part empty. In a few months that Baker St. house finally sold, but at a great loss. The selling price was only just enough to pay off the mortgage.

Luckily the Sacramento Street apartment had become vacant, just as the Baker Street house sale was complete. Daddy had told mama that when he came at Christmas time, he wanted a place with enough room and two bathrooms. He was delighted to learn that the one he had liked so much at 1455 Sacramento Street was the family's new home.

Though we missed Daddy, there were good times together. Often Mama packed a picnic and took us children to Golden Gate Park. We would sit by the statue of Schiller and Goethe. I wrote in my diary "I almost think I know Schiller and Goethe, when mama recites their poetry in German and tells us stories about them." I didn't know German, but "I felt it."

Our little family eagerly awaited Daddy's letters. Sometimes they contained a little extra money, but meanwhile Polhemus Company, where Daddy had worked but which he still represented in Guatemala, sent his retainer check promptly the first of every month.

On October 24th, 1929 the Wall Street crash occurred. Young as we were it was impossible to escape consciousness of the situation.

I wrote in my diary, "I think of that man we met in Los Angeles, Mr. Hansen; he was always talking about his stocks. He must be sad."

But Malcolm and I did not connect the market and stocks with our family. The depression did not seem to affect us.

1932 – 1933

For the first two years that Daddy was gone the depression didn't seem to affect us–not till a small commuter plane from Los Angeles crashed before landing near San Francisco. Aboard that plane was the owner of the firm that sent our monthly check, Mr. Polhemus. All aboard were killed.

As soon as she knew what had happened, Mama sent condolences and flowers to Mrs. Polhemus. Mama was terribly sorry for the family, However, she didn't really worry about Daddy's stipend. Certainly the company would go on, and Arthur would still represent them in Guatemala. No, she didn't worry until the phone rang one day as we were planning to go out on one of our Golden Gate Park picnics.

Mama put the picnic basket down to answer. She sat heavily on the chair by the phone as she listened to that message that would so change our lives.

"It's not coming? Not at ALL?" We children watched anxiously as our mother listened to the person on the other end. "Well, I guess somehow I will have to manage; thank you so much for letting me know. I can try to make plans while I wait to see what Arthur is going to do." Her goodbye had a slight tremble.

As best she could Mama explained to her young children now six and nine that there would be no more checks each month. There was nothing! "But don't worry children, your mamita will figure out something."

"Oh Mama, you are so smart, I'll pray to St. Anthony, he helps poor people."

"Oh are we poor?" Malcolm chimed in.

"No, no children, things will be alright, there all sorts of things I can do. Anyway, maybe Daddy will be able to soon send a little more from his Import Export agency."

Mama lost no time in rearranging our lives. Within two days the Examiner carried an ad "Room for rent, working woman only." When the first inquiry came, mama was not as frightened, as she had been the time she had rented out a room here to that nice Mrs. Kennedy. Adelita had become Adela again, strong Germanic, no longer submissive, dependant Latin Adelita.

The first to take a room was Dorothy Crowley. She had an important position at the board of trade. Miss Crowley was dressed appropriately for business, but her tailored clothes had softening feminine touches, a small ruffle at the throat, a handsome pin on her lapel. Later we grew to admire Dorothy's precision and fullness of speech. She chose her words rather than just tumbling them out.

My mother showed her both rooms, but when Dorothy saw the one with a view of trees, she said, "I spent my childhood in the Sierras and I love greenery. I'll take this one."

Dorothy was to become our lifelong friend. She went through it all with us. The only problem we ever had was with her boyfriend Tommy, later her husband. Tommy loved to cook and even did a sumptuous Thanksgiving dinner one year. However he would try to take over some times. Mama was fiercely protective of the parts of the apartment that had been left to her and her children.

The second girl taking a room was bouncy, redheaded Evelyn Strohm. She paid three months in advance, and explained with a laugh, "Times are getting so bad; I want to be sure if I lose my job that I'll have a roof over my head."

Before the two girls moved in, my mother completely resettled us. She moved Malcolm into a tiny room, just big enough for a bed and dresser. She had used the little room for storage, including two beds that could be raised to an upright position. They could easily be moved on their sturdy rollers. These two beds mama moved to the living room, where she and I could sleep when they were pulled down to horizontal. During the day they were raised and covered with attractive slips mama had made. No one would be the wiser—that the living room now served a dual purpose, bedroom and parlor.

The large dining room and the kitchen remained as our private quarters. But a one-purpose room was a luxury we could no longer afford. The rent the two girls paid did not even cover our rent. There was barely enough for food and transportation; but not enough for doctors—God forbid we get sick My school tuition had been paid for the whole year, and my uniforms were all purchased and ready for the coming school year. But somehow my mother Adela had to figure out how to fill the gap in income that had come so suddenly. She remembered what she had said to the Polhemus secretary, "I will have to make plans while I wait to see what Arthur will do."

I was old for my years so mama felt she could talk to me. One day she said, "I wish your Daddy would write and tell me, what's happening." The next day I was delighted to find a letter from Guatemala when I went as always to our box in the lobby. Mama pulled out the thin airmail sheet and read me the letter.

"My beloved Moyia; (His nickname for her.)

Apparently Hamburger Polhemus Company is breaking up. They are not even paying drafts against them that they owe. I have sent a cable asking for details and an explanation. I was worried when you wrote me that they had stopped your monthly checks.

Meanwhile I sent a cable to Garland Petroleum Co., one of my best clients, asking them, as a special favor, to send you $150.00 advance on my future commissions. I myself have nothing right now. So be very careful if they do send the $150.00. It may be a while before there is more. I have a few more commissions floating around but wholesalers don't pay me a commission till they themselves are paid for the goods shipped to my customer.."

He continued with family news and a few more business details.

Now mama knew she just had to figure a way to close the gap in income. "What can I do besides being a wife and mother?" she asked herself. Then she envisioned dozens and dozens of dresses she had made for Maria, her little sister-in-law, for herself, for friends, and finally the dresses for her three brides maids and her own wedding gown. She had learned the basics of sewing as a very little girl in the Convent of the Assumption, in Lyon, Nicaragua. Also, she had spent a great deal of time with her Tia Madelina, sister to the teacher Arcilia and the ever-sad tia Sulema. The three aunts belonged to a part of the family who were not affluent. Sewing or teaching was the only way a genteel female of limited means could earn a living.

Then she remembered how she had worked for Madame Nicolini that year after Mary was born. Adelita was no career woman. She had taken the sewing job with the couturier, only to shame Arthur into getting a regular job, and forget his mania of working for himself. Just as soon as he was established with Polhemus, she had resigned the sewing job. However, she had a strange feeling that he would have liked her to keep working. Rosa was there to take care of baby Mary. But Adelita would not harbor such thoughts. A lady would expect her husband to support her. As his wife she should be his hostess, his love, mother to his children. Work was for lower class women who HAD to. But now Adela Suhr Nicol HAD to work.

So another ad went into the Examiner, "Dressmaking and Alterations, experienced seamstress." And then she began to worry. When mama couldn't stand it another minute, dreading that the phone would ring with a customer, she went to see Mrs. Schwarz, the dressmaker who lived in the next apartment.

My mother barely knew her neighbor, a widowed single mother. However, Mrs. Schwartz's little boy Teddy and her Mary were the same age and played together in the yard. The women had had the usual mama conversations.

Now Mrs. Schwartz with her stolid German accent tried to calm her neighbor's fears. "Don't be foolish!" she chided. "You are good with the sewing. I see how you dress that Mary, and I suppose you make all your own nice dresses."

"Yes." Adela admitted. "But it is another thing sewing for other people and getting paid for it. I have always sewn for other people, but never received any pay for it. Well" she added "I did work for Madame Nicolini, where I had supervision; if I had a question there was always someone to ask."

"Just think that you will be doing them a favor." Mrs. Schwartz countered. "With times so bad, everyone is having things fixed, or lengthened, or turned around. Nobody throws clothes away any more. Tell you what, I have more work right now than I can do." And then she slapped her hands together,

"Ahch!!" another idea. "Mrs. Hart upstairs is a dressmaker. She doesn't have a sign like I do, because her apartment is in back. But I know she has more than she can do. I'll ask her if she will give you a few little jobs."

So it was that my mother was launched into business before anyone had a chance to answer her ad. Both dressmakers were delighted with her work, and immediately gave her more. So, when the first customer came in answer to her ad, mama could overcome her still present fear by assuring herself, "I have been sewing for money. My neighbors like my work."

That first customer, a curt, businesslike woman in her mid thirties, wanted a simple wool dress. With the wool material, she brought a pattern, all the necessary threads, zipper, and bindings. She told my mother that she had been apprehensive about trying out a new dressmaker; but she was desperate to have her dress made up.

Her former seamstress had left town to be near her son, who was stationed at one of the CCC (Civilian Conservation Corps.)

camps. In 1932 Roosevelt had established CCC to train some of the 12 million unemployed civilians. They were trained to work in construction of public works, to assist in natural disasters, and taught skills useful for future employment.

The two women discussed the time of the first fitting, and as Adela said goodbye, she was already wondering where she would cut out the dress, where she would put her machine, in short where her workroom was to be. The sewing she had done for the two dressmakers had been mostly handwork.

Now my professional mother needed to spread out, have a table for cutting, and get some order. She was really in business. Ah! Why not use the dining room? The large table was just right for cutting. So she cleared it and opened up the pattern envelope. She carefully laid out the pieces and with relief saw that it was a simple, well explained pattern, not one of those dreadful French concoctions.

By the time Malcolm and I arrived from school, four hours later, mama had the soft woolen material all pinned and cut. She interrupted her work to give us a snack and listen to our school happenings.

The first fitting went smoothly, as did the second. Finally the finished dress was presented to a no longer curt lady. She was delighted, and assured Mrs.Nicol that she would highly recommend her.

Many others followed that first customer, and ever more challenging work.

There were even a few of the complicated French patterns.

Mama no longer needed an ad; word of mouth brought her all the work she could do. She told the two of us," I wish I had little tooth picks to prop open my eyes. I am so tired."

But that sad complaint did not get through to me. I felt unloved with mama's busyness, and her often screaming at us. So I planned to run away. I had always been complimented on my dancing, had even been in programs put on by the Latin American colony. I packed some costumes in a little suitcase, and bought a package of needles which I put in the suitcase.. I guess I thought sewing was important. Anyway I was ready to go out the door when Evelyn Strohm came out of her room, "What are you doing Mary?"

"I am running away, Mama doesn't love me. I can get a job dancing."

"Come in my room, let's talk." And Evelyn put her arm around my shoulder and sat me down on her bed. After half an hour she had persuaded me running away was not a good idea. "Your mother loves you, it is just that she is so tired and worried. You would be doing a terrible thing to her."

What would have happened if that dear girl had not "caught" me?

I never told mama, nor did Evelyn tattle on me. Mama went on with her work, never knowing.

The night hours were best for work, it was quiet, we were in bed, and her little machine whirred away almost continuously. For several years my mother Adela did all her sewing on a small Wilcox and Gibbs chain-stitch machine. Every seam had to be done twice, so that the chain would not rip out. She would have liked a rugged commercial machine, but buying one was out of the question. If she could only sew faster, turn out more work. Her present earnings were just not enough. Every month she ran a little behind, in spite of the room rents and her ever increasing clientele.

Mama always shared Daddy's correspondence with me and with Malcolm if he was interested. In their letters Arthur and Adela discussed finances at length. She told of her financial worries. He told of his contacts in Germany, England, and of course in the United States, where he had worked till leaving to make his fortune in Guatemala. It had seemed so hopeful in 1929 when he'd left; financial backing could be had for almost any idea that gave promise. But how that had changed with the 30's depression.

Mama kept begging Daddy to come back, "You could easily find another job with your years of experience. Your success selling American exports when we were first married, the contacts made in England, Germany and here during the Polhemus years, all this makes you valuable to any number of companies."

But Daddy felt that as an employee he could never have the life style he so longed for. In Latin America he was able to get credit. Yes, Adelita was right, he did have contacts in Germany, England and the United States.

As their representative he could sell their products to a wholesaler or a service that used those products. However, very often the Latin American client did not pay Daddy till the products they had purchased were sold, invoiced and reimbursed. Meanwhile Daddy had to take care of the manufacturer's invoice. For these payments he needed to borrow. His "capital" was all hand to mouth.

So Daddy had to have capital, all from loans, with which to pay the invoice from the company he represented. Then he received his commission. If enough commissions were coming in, which several years later they did, He could begin to repay his loans. In the meantime he couldn't move, not even think of coming back to the States.

It had seemed so hopeful in 1929 when he left; financial backing could be had for almost any idea that gave promise. Now, only in Latin America could he get sufficient credit.

In one letter he said "It isn't just here that there is a depression, it is world wide, darling," But he added, "It just can't last."

Arthur did not stop at Export/Import, he had other projects.

He was way ahead of his time in another endeavor. He felt if coffee were to be roasted and freshly ground, then presented to the public in special coffee shops, or through regular markets, it would be a great success. But no one would listen; "The supermarkets would squelch such an enterprise. They want to sell their own coffee."

Years later a little company in Washington State, Starbucks proved that it *was* a great idea, even Safeway sells freshly roasted "Starbucks" in their markets.

Daddy had come very close to success when a German plantation owner liked his idea of roasting and selling premium coffee direct to the public. But just as they were to terminate the deal, a bank where the man had $50,000 crashed. The German assured Arthur that if and when he got either that or some other money, he would back him; meanwhile—sorry! >>>

And so month after month, hope after hope became disappointment. As Adela described their crowded living conditions, the eternal beans and lettuce she served, because they were the cheapest and most nutritious food available, Arthur wrote back of his own troubles.

He said, *"I can no longer afford the nice room with a private bath, where I have been living. It was in the pension run by two delightful old ladies. They presented wonderful food, graciously served. Instead I have had to move to my brother Henry's house. There is no guest room, so they have put me in the baby's room. They did take the child into their own bedroom. However, all the baby's things remain there, and periodically a servant comes in to get clean diapers and leaves the dirty ones till laundry time. The smell is getting me down. Do you think I would have left my comfort for this, if it wasn't that I can no longer afford the $50 a month I was paying?"*

Even after more than a year of effort on both their parts, the situation was bad. Arthur was only able to send Adela an occasional check; $25.00 one month, $50.00 a couple of months later. His Adelita ran ever deeper in debt. Did she miss him? I don't think she had time or energy to miss Daddy, money worries sat too heavily on her.

It began with the little corner grocery, where she had a charge account. I was usually sent for the groceries if there wasn't too much to carry. When the Polhemus checks suddenly stopped coming, we kept charging; we had to eat; but so did the grocery man. After two months, credit stopped, so I was sent to another store—there was a grocery on every corner. It was easy for an 11 year old to say, "Oops, I don't have quite enough money, can I pay you next time?"

Was this an adventure for an 11 year old? No, just a member of the family getting what was needed. Also I really believed soon Daddy would be sending enough money and I would be able to go pay the grocery stores.

And always it was me who was sent to the meat market for the little bit we could buy. The butcher gave me a little extra, and a sausage just for me because I smiled so brightly.

1934

Then the rent began to get behind. Mama would miss one month, barely be able to pay the next, then two months would pass with only a note of apology. A dear old Jewish lady named Mrs. Jones owned the Sacramento Street building. She was patient for six months, but finally insisted my mother move. "You can give me back rent whenever you are able; but I just must get my apartment back and rent to someone who can pay.

Mama immediately wrote Daddy the bad news, his return letter was almost like a cry of anguish;

"What more can go wrong! Terrible news, you're being asked to move. You tell me that it is definite that you must vacate your apartment by the end of next month. If it is inevitable I hope at least you don't have to lose your furniture. I will pray you find a suitable place. Maybe you could find an apartment manager's job, and thus have a free apartment. Anyway I hope soon soon I can send you enough money that you can stop worrying all the time."

We were being evicted! My main emotion was concern for mama "Why don't we say a prayer to St. Joseph. He is the patron of shelter, mama!" Sure enough, St. Joseph came through. We both were certain that the saint had interceded and caused Arthur to receive his first big commission check from Owens Illinois Glass Company, which he represented in Guatemala. He had landed the beer bottling account at one of the local breweries. The commission, which he sent directly to Mama was enough to pay three months rent for a nice bright apartment a few blocks away on Washington and Jones.

The Nicol family would be in the same neighborhood for Mama's sewing customers, and we two would still be near our friends. Mama was glad for her Mary, who so enjoyed the library close by, and for Malcolm who had a bunch of little boys he played with on an empty lot nearby. They played baseball in baseball season, football in football season. Yes, the move to 1335 Washington Street offered hope for better times. In fact each move we made was for the better. Here on Washington we didn't have to have roomers.

In my weekly letters to Daddy I would beg him to come home. I adored my father, and had faith that he could do anything.

However, there was still not enough money for him to make a trip north. Furthermore he couldn't leave the business that seemed at last to have promise. He had been gone five years. Excerpts from letters June 1934 to December 1935 give a picture of his life and hopes.

"June 5, 1934 to December 31, 1935

October 6, 1934

You tell me that Mary entertained a few friends alone in the apartment, cooked the dinner and was a successful hostess. You had taught her how to do things, so went out and let her try her wings. I should have loved to see my little daughter being "Dama de Casa" (Lady of the house). God willing we will be together soon.

Today I received a confirming letter from Owens Illinois Glass Company, confirming that they will send you all my commissions. I hope you will soon be receiving something worth while. I will try to increase the sale of their products, all the commissions are yours, no matter how big they get.

In one letter Daddy felt we should not be accepting money from cousin Carmela, who had married a rich Mr. Cohn. But we desperately needed every penny. Mr. Cohn would hug me and give me $5.00. "Take your mama to the opera." Ha! Buy food. But Mr. Cohn thought we really went to the opera.

Although Mama had showed herself capable of managing under almost impossible circumstances, Daddy still felt he had to give fatherly advice to her. January 15, 1935 he wrote,

"I have a new account that will pay more. I told them to send you the commissions–amounts $50 and at times $100. But because you are receiving more, don't go paying off debts, keep it for your daily expenses. In fact, if you get enough, you should start building a reserve of about $100, which shouldn't be touched unless there is

nothing else. But if more does come in, then you can start paying debts."

But three months later he wrote a most discouraging letter about world financial events.

March 5, 1935

"*Business has taken a different turn lately. Germany is giving enormous discounts for exports and has freed millions of credits against them by other countries. That is they allow drawing against these funds to pay for German exports. This results in everyone being in a rush to sell marks, and as there are so many, they offer them at 30% discount. This results in German merchandise being extremely cheap. Selling American or other non–German merchandise is extremely difficult. England is lowering the pound externally to the point that English merchandise could compete with the German. It is a war without cannons, but a war nevertheless.*"

Mama had not taken any new work in anticipation of the move. She told her customers she would let them know when she was settled. With three months rent paid, Adela could catch her breath a little. She was determined not to get any deeper in debt.

Mama had just about put everything away and was ready to start calling her old customers, when one of the little servant girls from Nicaragua, who periodically came to visit Niña Adelita, told her that she was working in a dress factory. She was been paid more than mama earned with her dressmaking.

Mama wondered what she was doing sticking to her home dressmaking. But the children were a problem. Though we were 8 and 11 now, she just couldn't leave us alone all day, especially with summer coming up. It was getting increasingly difficult to confine Malcolm's activities to home. On Sacramento Street there was a huge yard where the boys played football in fall and baseball in spring. But Malcolm kept begging to go to an empty lot several blocks away where there were older boys. The factory work would be so much better than home dressmaking; but she had to find a way to have us supervised.

Just then, one of her neighbors, Mrs. Hoffler, a divorcee with a daughter my age, told Mama of a small boarding school on the Peninsula, "Little Oxford." She had arranged to send her daughter, Hope there. My mother phoned the owner, an Englishwoman, and made an appointment for the next Saturday. The three of us took a bus to Palo Alto, and were impressed with Little Oxford School. It was housed in a lovely old mansion, surrounded by a flower filled garden. There were about 20 children in residence, mostly about Malcolm's age.

The owner described the activities that kept her charges busy and happy. Malcolm was apprehensive. He didn't like leaving mama. However, I was excited about the weekly movie, the row of individual wash basins off the "big girls'" room. But what I found really exciting was the ballroom dancing lessons every Friday night. "That's certainly English," remarked my mother. Malcolm saw nothing good in that!

"I must think about it." she told the English lady. I shall let you know by week's end whether or not the children will be enrolled." She must make sure she could actually get one of those factory jobs. But, she wasn't about to tell the snooty Englishwoman that. As far as the Little Oxford director knew, this was a lady from

San Francisco who needed a respite from children with summer coming up.

That Monday mama engaged one of her ex-servant girls to come and stay with us, while she went to apply at a factory. She returned with a work assignment starting a week from the next Monday.

Only assurance that he could take his precious Teddy Bear, Moolux, consoled Malcolm. As an eleven- year-old girl, I was more interested in which clothes I was to take. Preparing these took the rest of that week. Frantically my mother made a couple of summer dresses, mended, lengthened, re-trimmed, till her little girl was all ready for this new adventure.

Malcolm's things were carefully laundered—a scrub board and the kitchen sink was all Mama had— then checked for rips and tears. It was all packed into one of her old suitcases, the one with all the European labels on it.

Mama wondered how she would get down to the Peninsula with all the paraphernalia; then she remembered her good friends from Nicaragua who had just come to town. They were living in a family hotel near by and gladly lent her their car and chauffeur for the trip to Little Oxford.

I was glad to have had that experience, but it was pretty grim for my little brother. The English director—I don't recall her name— ran the school in typical English style. Appearances were what mattered. But there was never enough to eat. We older girls, about six of us, had a dormitory to ourselves. We were allowed to go to the movies on one night; on Fridays the dancing teacher came for the manners and ballroom lesson. But the young ones, age eight like my brother were kept in a small space, not allowed to make noise, and threatened if they started to cry.

Every weekend Malcolm begged mama to take us out of there. One weekend he was in absolute hysterics, and when I confirmed to our mother that really the little ones were mistreated, kept hungry and not allowed to play, or to run. I could not protect Malcolm, the older and younger pupils were kept separate. Only on weekends could he tell me of the difference in our treatment. Mama phoned the head mistress and told her the children would not be returning.

There was an awful fuss trying to get our luggage and things back; the woman insisted the family had contracted for the entire summer. She said that Mrs. Nicol owed her for the remaining time. A lawyer friend of ours spoke to the English woman; he threatened to expose her treatment of the small children in her care. It ended there but mama was never able to retrieve the suitcase or the clothes that had been left at Little Oxford.

So mama had to resign the factory job, and try to resume her home dressmaking. Her life was busy but peaceful for the next couple of years, that is, till Miss Walker, the exotic dancer who lived downstairs came into our lives.

Malcolm kept talking about the beautiful blonde lady who lived downstairs, but my mother and I didn't meet Miss Walker till she rang the bell and inquired whether the seamstress sewed dance costumes.

"Yes indeed." My mother answered. "I have made many costumes for Mary-Spanish, Gypsy, and some fairy costumes." Mama had made these for all the little girls I played with on Jackson Street. We had flitted all over the landlord's lawn; diaphanous capes waving from our shoulders and gauzy wings trembling as we leapt all over the yard.

Further, Mama had made costumes for herself and for Arthur. They attended many masquerades in the early years of their marriage. The soul of the Spanish Colony was nourished by parties. The handsome Nicol couple was one of the brightest lights of that luminous group. So Adela felt competent to make costumes for Miss Walker.

However, although Miss Walker was glad to hear of Adela's experience making costumes; with a slight cough she said, "Well, mine may be a little different."

Mama told me later that she was so glad we weren't home. She would have been even more embarrassed, fearing we'd come in and see Miss Walker naked. Naked she had to be, fitted to the costumes required by law in those days—the law stipulated nipples and pelvic area must be covered. My mother had taught us to call it "La cosita" "the little thing." The word served for both male and female parts.

Well, such delicacies were forgotten in fitting the spectacular "exotic" dancer. But Miss Walker paid well, so delicacy was something Adela couldn't afford. Luckily the fitting was done before we came home.

Malcolm and I became friendly with the beautiful lady; she even taught me some of her dances, greatly, greatly cleaned up for sure. It was a nice relationship till she moved in with us!

Miss Walker had to have some sort of minor operation and

asked Adela if she could stay with us temporarily, when she left the hospital. She would pay, of course. Well, it was fine till she started leaving her reading matter all over, and my mother found me eagerly reading one of the magazines. I couldn't figure what my mother's fuss was all about; I didn't understand the jokes, or the articles. There were pictures of pretty ladies in funny positions; I just thought they were silly.

However, my mother certainly did understand. She immediately told Miss Walker that she would have to go back to her own apartment, "You are much stronger now; and take all these magazines!"

Miss Walker left in a blonde hair tossing fury. We were forbidden to visit her. That was the end of that, thought my mother.

The end, that is, till Adela Nicol got a summons to small claims court. Miss Walker was suing Adela Nicol for "throwing her out, and shaking dust into her apartment below." Mother had shaken her mop, but had been careful to look whether the windows below were closed.

I considered myself a young lady—at 13 I was" grown-up." I tried to look sophisticated, even sneaked makeup once in a while. But when we were to appear in court, mama dressed me in flat shoes with socks, a large straw hat and a sailor dress. I was furious, but calmed down when my mother explained that her defense for asking Miss Walker to leave was that she filled the house with filthy magazines and the defendant had an innocent little girl to protect, as well as a young son. God knows what the dancer might teach him.

Miss Walker, on the other hand wore an outfit that assured losing her case. Black net stockings, a tight skirt, and a blouse that emphasized what made the exotic dancer exotic.

So, by mother winning the case, her Mary's purity was saved, and Adela did not have to pay a fine for throwing a poor sick lady out of her home. But fear replaced the friendship that had existed with the interesting lady downstairs. My mother knew she would have to move.

She barely was able to pay the rent each month; how on earth could she find enough to pay first and last month's rent for a new apartment? Just then, one of the O'Connor girls, Mary phoned. They had remained friends ever since the time when my mother had come to the O'Connors when she arrived in San Francisco. From their house she had been married, Mary O'Connor was one of her bride's maids.

Mama told Mary of her worry about Miss Walker—some pretty tough looking characters visited the dancer..

"But I don't see how I can get the first and last months rent for a new place."

"That's no problem," countered Mary "Grace and I would be glad to lend you a hundred dollars.

That is how we came to move to the apartment on Washington and Polk, and pay four months in advance. The rent was $20.00. From that apartment I had my first date, my mother cut down on her sewing, and life began to look a little better.

Only a decision mama had to make about Malcolm marred the happiness of our new quarters. About a month before we left the other Washington Street apartment, Malcolm had again wanted to wander further than the Sacramento back yard where he had played before. He had discovered a bunch of older boys who played in a lot on California Street. A large house had been torn down, leaving only the cave-like basement. Here the boys held their secret meetings. When my brother wandered in one day instead of chasing him away, the leader took a fancy to the ten year old kid.

For a while Malcolm said nothing about his new "friends"; but one day he blurted out, "Mama, the leader of the gang on the California Street empty lot likes me. He says I am young, but I can be the gang's mascot."

The shock of hearing the word "gang" moved mama to immediate action. She sought the advice of a priest at Old Saint Mary's church. "I have very little money; a boarding school is impossible." Father McNally immediately calmed her with the following information.

"Mrs. Nicol, there is a school in Marin County, "St Vincent's School for Boys" It was established for lower income families who needed a disciplined atmosphere for young boys. It is not a reform school; in fact it has saved many boys from reform school."

"But what does it cost?" asked Adela.

"Whatever you can afford, or nothing if your income warrants it."

With Father Mc Nally's help, mother was able to arrange for Malcolm's acceptance, settle for a small monthly payment, and make an appointment to register her son at St. Vincent's. All that remained was finding someone to take her and Malcolm to the school in Marin County, near the town of San Rafael. Again the O'Connors came to the rescue. Bert O'Connor offered to drive Adela and Malcolm there on a Tuesday, when he could take off from work.

Bert piled Malcolm's things into the trunk of his car; placed a silent, frowning boy in the back seat, his friend Adela in the passenger seat, and off they went, on the Ferry and then onto a road in Marin County, that later became highway 101.

The school was not hard to find. When they were nearing San Rafael, there on the right side of the road was the tall church spire of the school's chapel. Bert turned right and drove down a long avenue with tall Eucalyptus trees on either side. At the end of the road was the spacious campus with several buildings surrounding the chapel—really a church. A wealthy donor, with a taste for authentic architecture was most likely responsible for the imposing building.

Bert immediately spotted a sign saying "Office." They were expected, and immediately escorted first to the dormitory, assigned to Malcolm. Here his possessions were deposited into a spacious locker.

Mama and Bert were impressed with the tour of the dining room, class rooms, recreation room, with various games spread out on tables; no T V in 1933. The football field was the only thing that caused a spark of interest in Malcolm.

Finally it was time to say goodbye. Bert took Malcolm's hand, "Good luck boy; you will be glad some day." Mama, holding back tears, hugged her son. Then, for the first time since they had arrived, Malcolm spoke, "I didn't think you would do this to me!"

"It is because I love you, Malcolm." She hugged him again, Bert opened the car door and mother got into the car. As they drove off they saw Malcolm walking away with the registrar who had given them the tour.

I had not come because it was a school day; but mama gave me all the details, between bouts of crying. All the next week she kept thinking when and how she could visit Malcolm.

The registrar had told them that if a boy behaved himself during the week, he could have visitors on the weekend. Mama wanted to go every weekend—she knew Malcolm would behave—but the trip was long, first by city bus to the Ferry station, and another bus to Northern Marin. The bus did go into St. Vincent's, but still it was a three hour round trip.

However, my mother found that this was not the only way of getting there. Several times one of the O'Connor girls drove us there. Being able to visit more often helped her adjust to the difficult decision she had made.

Malcolm stayed at St. Vincent's two years. Besides an excellent program of regular studies, the boy learned a great deal about gangs. Some of his fellow schoolmates had been yanked out of a gang life by wise parents, who had seen St. Vincent's as a salvation.

My mother had never liked having her little son away at St. Vincent's. The last time she had visited she felt Malcolm had finally become more responsible. He actually thanked her for having sent him there. So she put her arm around his shoulder and said to her twelve year old son, "I think you should come home now. St, Bridget's parish has a good school and is close to our apartment. It might be a little crowded but we three can manage.

So Malcolm was enrolled at St. Brigit's into the sixth grade. He walked to and from school, and had to work much too hard under the stern rule of Sister Sophia, ever to think of gangs or wandering around.

Besides his studies, Malcolm took a job selling newspapers on a corner assigned him, on Sutter and Franklin streets. One of his schoolmates, Edward McGinnis, drove Malcolm to his corner every day in his family's chauffeured car. Edward was driven to and from school daily, and could tell the chauffeur to make a stop for his friend Malcolm.

Daddy's letters in 1936 more often now contained a check, or notice that one of the accounts was sending a commission. It was usually $100 in a month. In the letter below he joked about a 42 cent shortage, before telling about Uncle Jack.

"Enclosed are 8 checks amounting to $99.58. I hope the 42 cents wont make you short."

" So Uncle Jack has been telling you tales about me. The dear man advises you to divorce me and marry someone who can really support you. Then you write that maybe I want to be free–WHAT FOR? It seems strange that Uncle Jack should talk of separation unless you have said something that made him think you are dissatisfied with your marriage. Well I guess you are NOT happy with your union–NO WAY!"

But he ended with "Maybe it is best not to divorce, Moycia. I do believe something good will come this year and your "poor" husband will be able to give you all you deserve. Hugs and Kisses....."

Letters from February to June brought ever larger checks,

especially the ones from Owens Illinois Glass Co. This account was to be for Adela exclusively; fortunately it increased each month.

With Malcolm back from St. Vincent's, the apartment on Washington and Polk Streets was proving to be crowded. With the added income, Adela was able to find and rent larger accommodations.

Our little family of three was soon installed in the best apartment we had ever had. Washington and Presidio had two bedrooms, a very large dining room, besides a breakfast nook in the spacious kitchen. The apartment was perfect for entertaining. Downstairs were the garages, upstairs a hard of hearing lady, and next door a dear older man who told us "Make all the noise you want; I love to hear young people having fun." From then on, till I graduated from High school, there were parties, many dates, and three romances, Fred Stevens, the Argentine Paco Gonzalez, and Mario Chacon from Costa Rica.

I always came in after a date, woke mama and told her all about the evening. She relived her own youth in my social life. Usually it was a matter of meeting and briefly chatting with the latest escort, and then hearing all about the date when I came home. Mama was more like a big sister now.

But this is Mama's story, only my final romance with my future husband, Russell Jones-belongs in her story three years later.

Those years still did not bring a trip home for Daddy. Frequent letters from the three of us kept him informed- my graduation and acceptance at U.C. Berkeley, Mama's sewing, and much about Malcolm.

MALCOLM

Daddy was always interested in both of us, but when his son started high school, my mother wanted to give him more details about school and his son's experience with business.

In September 1935, Malcolm commenced his four happy, successful high-school years. He had his own room, and his "dreadful" music; Bennie Goodman, the Dorseys, Satchemo—they all sound so mild today, but according to mother, they were works of the devil. She forgave his dreadful music because he was such a serious student at St. Ignatius High School.

Furthermore he was serious about his "business." Malcolm had sold The Saturday Evening Post when he was a very young boy-before he went to St. Vincent's. A distributor of the "Post" would meet the little boys assigned him, on a given corner; there he would hand out the allotted number of magazines to each boy.

What Malcolm did not deliver to one of his regular customers, because they had moved, or had not paid the bill, he would usually sell to someone who wanted to buy this week's Saturday Evening Post.

He had always kept in touch with his distributor, and when he returned to San Francisco, the ex boss approached his now teenaged salesman with an offer of a distributorship." But Mal, you will need a car." Impossible thought Malcolm. But when he told mama, she said "I will write your father, maybe he will help out."

In his return letter, Daddy did say he would send money enough for a little second hand car, but it would be a loan. Malcolm must learn to be a good businessman. And so it was his son acquired a wonderful little black sedan, with a rumble seat. He faithfully sent his father the agreed monthly payments and did well as a Saturday Evening Post Distributor. In his letters to Malcolm Daddy told him how proud he was of his businessman son.

But there was more than work and study. His social life was full. The little black car would daily be piled up with boys crowded inside and hanging on behind, or on the sides. It was a happy confusing sight.

Malcolm was invited to join the Assemblies. This time Adela could afford the initiation fee for these dances that had been established many years ago so that young people of "good" families would meet and form the associations that would last them the rest of their lives. At the assemblies, he met the only girl he was ever to love. Patty Deasy was the daughter of a judge. She and Malcolm went steady till he went into the Air Corps. Separation somehow ended the romance and Patty married a Naval Officer.

All during these four years, 1936 to 1939 Daddy's letters continued. Mama kept most of them. However correspondence from 1937 and 1938 are missing and only two for 1939, and one each for 1940 and 1941. To quote them best gives Mama's story.

June 7, 1939

Thank you for your "Happy Birthday" letter. Imagine I have reached forty years! I don't feel even thirty. The only present I received was from the family of the girl who works for me. It was a beautiful hand crocheted bedspread, all in one piece with a lining of fine silk.

This family, the Bocaleti's have been very kind to me. After Lucy had been my secretary for a couple of months, she brought a delicious dish her mother had made for me. I had been eating badly, only occasionally accepting invitations from my brothers and sister Mary. So I asked Lucy if her mother would consider having me as a paying guest for meals. She said gladly, so for six months I have been having all my meals at their house. It is a friendly atmosphere, Lucy's sixteen year old sister Carmen is always making us laugh, such a happy girl.

The weekly letters continued in the same vein, improving finances, and much talk of trusting God. December 29, 1940 was the last letter that year.

December 29, 1940

"I am so glad that the little money I sent the children allowed them to buy a few things they had wanted. I hope soon I can sent them more."

He went on to tell Adela news of the family and ended the letter with a reply to mama's asking him when he will come.

"You say that you believe that this next year we will see each other—øjala (maybe/hopefully). But at the moment I see nothing sure. I merely think, and know that if it is right for all of us it will be. Nothing can stop the power of God. I say, "If it is Right for us." I think that our reunion must occur when God wants. He will make it happen when it is right for us.

Thank you for the pictures. You are more beautiful than the picture—you're staying young and I am aging. Half my hair is now white. Hugs and kisses etc.

August 10, 1941

Mi Moycia Linda Querida: (All past letters said "Adorada"; Querida is just plain "dear"!)

I am glad the $124 cheque arrived in time to save the situation. I hope you will not continue having financial difficulties.

Since the first of August I had it in my head that your birthday was the 12ᵗʰ. But I went to look in my "birthdays" book and saw to my horror it was 7ᵗʰ. I hope the cable I immediately sent you arrived by the 7ᵗʰ. Forgive my bird brain–but you know my terrible memory.

He went on with inquiries about Malcolm. Daddy became increasingly interested in his son's progress, even to asking how tall he was and how much he weighed. He compared his youth with Malcolm's, saying at that age "I was already in love with Adelita; did she love me? " The letter ended, *Let's see what the next five years bring us. Hugs and kisses etc.*

There are two letters in 1942, quoted in the next chapter, "CHANGE"

CHAPTER VIII
CHANGE
TRIP TO MEXICO

As I sat there in the nursing home, taking notes of my mother's life, I asked her, "Mama, wasn't there anything else in your life except us, Malcolm and Mary? You had so much in your youth, Paris, Germany, your cousin Albert, and Herbert. How did we become your only interest?"

Then mama reminded me of our trip to Mexico. She said, "That trip brought back my past." I did recall that trip in 1939, just after my first semester at the University of California in Berkeley. It had been another example of how Mama was skilled at maneuvering toward a goal.

Adela's cousin Sarita, the one who had persuaded her to come to Paris in 1912, had always kept up her correspondence with her cousin. She had married the young man from Mexico. For years now she had begged Adela, she called her Adelita, to come to Mexico for a visit. It had been impossible financially, and time wise, besides Mama had to make a living. But now Adela figured how she could accomplish a trip to Mexico. First she wrote a letter to Arthur.

My darling Arthur, Moycio:

I am sure you remember cousin Sarita. For years she has been inviting me and the family to visit in Mexico City. I think a trip like this would be wonderful and educational for Mary and Malcolm. I myself could certainly use the rest, enjoy being waited on, and just relax talking about old times. I have figured out how we might be able to take this trip.

1. A friend of mine is sending her large car to Mexico with two drivers. To lessen her expense, she has let it be known that she would accept passengers in the back seat for a small fee.

2. If you could possibly send me two months of the $160.00 that you send monthly, I could manage the trip.

3. I could give up this apartment, put our things in storage, so have no rent to pay for the three vacation months.

She ended with bits of news and some loving words.

Arthur did send the double amount, and Adela plunged into her preparations; giving notice, giving up the apartment, putting everything in storage, buying necessary clothes, including something comfortable to wear for the long three day trip. She was informed that the young men driving did not intend to stop overnight, just keep going and take turns sleeping.

Finally, we three piled into the back seat of the large black Cadillac. It was a grueling trip! My mother, Malcolm and I were jammed into the back seat, the chauffeur and George Harris, who was to help with the driving as his share of the trip sat in the front seat. George was a fine artist, and wanted to study in Mexico. A day after we had started, I sat between the two men, and it was my job to see that the driver stayed awake. We drove for three days, day and night, stopping only for meals and cold drinks in the desert. My poor mother suffered from the heat and was exhausted. She had to spend a week in bed when we arrived. My brother, who was already six feet tall, went through an agony of cramps in that back seat.

But for me, hungry to know, to see, and to experience, they were three days of exhilaration, especially when I was talking to George the artist. His conversation showed me a world of which I had no experience––the world of artists, of liberals, of tearing apart the fabric of security in things as they have always been. My mother did not approve of my semi–flirting with George. She felt it was disloyal to Russell, with whom I was supposed to be in love. "He is such a nice boy." She chided me.

But we finally arrived at Mexico City. The chauffeur immediately drove us to 45 Calle Tecal. There behind a tall metal wall stood the handsome stone mansion. It had been the British Embassy, until the Britishers needed more spacious quarters, and sold the house to the Solorzanos, my mother's cousins.

The life in that house was wonderful at first-- fantastic meals, servants all over the place, lovely gardens, and interesting trips by chauffeured car. However, I found my cousin Idalia an odd girl, I felt no rapport. Her mother, my mother's cousin was a very strange woman. She kept her daughter, Idalia, who was my age, a complete child. She still played with dolls, even though she was at that exciting "hungry for growth and excitement" age, nineteen. Her life was supposed to be fulfilled with her studies and trips to the museums with her governess. I went along with Idalia, and did enjoy the exhibits, and the explanations given by her knowledgeable teacher.

Meanwhile my mother had her needed rest, and spent hours with Sarita recalling the joys of their youth. Right now, however, both Sarita and her husband, Ernesto were having a problem with their son Rene. He had married a girl from a very good old Mexican family; her grandfather had been president of Mexico. However, the family had come into hard times, so the Solorzanos did not think she would financially add to the union, though socially her family was certainly an asset.

So far it had only been a civil marriage, and Rene was still at home. This was the custom in Latin America; civil then religious ceremonies. Rene's parents threatened that if he went through with the church wedding, they would cut him off.

The poor young man was going through hell. I shall never forget his anguished words to me, "Wait till you want to marry your Russell, then you will see what a Latin family can be. Mary, they own us, we have no rights until they die." Little did I know how prophetic were his words!

But he did have the courage to go through with the wedding. I think eventually his family relented; but relations between the two families were always cold. The whole affair did not actually spoil the visit for my mother, she still enjoyed talking of old times with her cousin, and having the rest she so badly needed. However, she dared not speak of the problem with their son; only tried to persuade them that things would turn out well.

Malcolm, on the other hand was miserable the entire time. The altitude of Mexico City wore him out. He remembered how the Olympic teams had had breathing and energy problems in that altitude. So this potential athlete, who loved football and had hoped to gain weight during the summer, instead lost weight, and lacked the energy to do the calisthenics he had planned to do.

My mother was always interested in politics, but I was innocent of nations and their maneuverings. I did not even realize the significance of the two men who came to the house one day, directly from president Roosevelt. The Camancho presidential election was approaching, and apparently the United States government favored Camancho. My uncle was the go between. I was asked to do the typing for some documents pertaining to their negotiations. It was all very hush hush; they did not even dare hire a secretary. I just typed what was dictated, but did not understand what was going on. It didn't occur to me to ask why Roosevelt sent two men to talk about or negotiate about the Mexican election.

Camancho got in all right; it would have been strange had he not, seeing that many of the voting booths for the opposing candidate had machine guns planted in front. We saw busloads of peons brought in to the city to vote, plenty of strong pulque, their cheap liquor, provided. The buses carried huge signs, "Viva Camancho." although I argued with my uncle about the injustice of the very rich and the very poor, it did not occur to me to see anything wrong in this rigged election; after all, I was told, the good guys were seeing to it that the bad guys didn't get in.

A month before we were to return to the States, Cousin Ernesto offered to send my mother to Guatemala to visit Arthur. Mama was apprehensive, but eager to see her husband. However, when they phoned Guatemala and talked to him, Adelita and the family were surprised to hear Arthur protest, "It is not a good idea for Adelita to come. There is no place for her to stay. I live in a small room at my brother's house. I could not afford to put her up in a hotel, and none of the other relatives has room. It will be best if my wife and the children return to United States. We will see each other some other time."

As she had done all her married life, Mrs. Nicol took Arthur Nicol at his word. It was inconvenient for him—so life goes on. She was disappointed of course, but proceeded to make arrangements for our return to San Francisco.

My mother had already written her friend Dorothy Thomas, asking her to find an apartment. Housing was tight because of the war, but Dorothy wrote back that she had secured a one–bedroom apartment on Pine Street. Oh how that address was to cause trouble for me!

For our return to San Francisco, with the help of Cousin Ernesto, we made arrangements with a young Mexican–American who was returning to the States. Ernesto checked his references carefully. When the young man, Pedro Guzman came for an interview, we all immediately liked his quiet humor. He was casually dressed, open shirt, slightly worn slacks, and a crazy squashed hat, which he immediately took off on entering the house. "He is more

American than Mexican," remarked Cousin Ernesto, who always wore buttoned down shirt and tie.

After about an hour of pleasant conversation, he suggested we take a look at his vehicle. We were all Ohs and Ahhs at the spacious Dodge station wagon. There was plenty of room for Malcolm's long legs, and my mother could even stretch out on the last seat in back.

So three days later, after prolonged hugging goodbyes, we boarded the van. Pedro, seeing that especially "la Señora Adelita" was comfortable, got in last. We finally took off and headed north.

It was a comfortable, many stops trip, nothing spectacular to tell. The events once we reached San Francisco make a better story. A story that changed all three lives, my mother's, mine and even Malcolm's.

A DIVORCE , A MARRIAGE

Sally Stanford—how could one of the top Madams of San Francisco enter our lives? The apartment Dorothy had procured for us was on Pine Street, right next door to Sally's famous "house." For a while we were not aware of our "interesting" location. I thought there were only two problems with our new home; first the fact that I had to sit in the closet to study because it was the only quiet spot; second I had terrible fights with Malcolm who would monopolize the bathroom and delay my doing my makeup when I had a date with Russell. He hated to be kept waiting. All this was the least of the Pine street problems. It began with my engagement.

On one of our dates, when he had parked in front of my apartment at the end of the evening Russell pulled a little jewelry box out his pocket. Characteristically, he just handed it to me and said "Open it."

There was a simply set ring with an enormous diamond. The gem had been in the family many years. His grandfather had acquired it from a client as payment of a debt. It must have been a whopper of a debt, a four-carat debt. Russell had had it set at Shreve's, and chuckled with delight at my squeals. Best we were not in a restaurant. Some sqishy, passionate kisses, and squeals, and it was time to go up to the apartment.

When I let myself in, only Malcolm was up. He was excited by my ring, but said, "Better wait till morning to tell mama."

The next morning, as we sat at the breakfast table, I suddenly stuck my left hand out, without a word. No "O's", no squeals, just "Oh dear, what is that for?" Then tears, and reminders that Russell had lost his job, what was he thinking of? I hope the Joneses are not going to start putting announcements in the paper."

What a letdown! The morning ended with my making a promise that Russell's family would not put an announcement in the papers, that I was to keep this engagement secret. But a worse problem replaced my disappointment. Our address, next door to Sally Stanford was the problem because of an invitation to the Roth wedding.

Russell's cousin Spencer Grant was engaged to Brenice Roth, daughter of the Matson shipping family. Because Russell's Aunt Marie, very socially conscious, was ashamed of my address on Pine Street right next door to the Madame Sally Stanford's "house, an invitation could not be sent directly to me. Because of our "red light." neighborhood Aunt Marie had the invitation for me, Russell's intended, mailed to her address.

I was not even aware of all this, just excited to be going to a fancy wedding. My mother bought me a wonderful brown hat with a beaver like finish. At the time Aunt Marie didn't say anything, but later told me she felt it looked like "A maid's day off hat." Later I understood that in that San Francisco society. A tiny "pill box" would have been correct.

I cannot say I had a wonderful time at the wedding; I guess I was trying too hard to do and say the right thing. I had been to the Sacred Heart Convent, graduated, and learned the manners, the dignity that the daughters of European royalty had learned at European Sacred Hearts. But this San Francisco society froze me inside. .

But worse yet was Russell's continuing objection to my address. I discussed it with mama, who agreed with Russell that living next to a house of ill repute was not good. Mama too was socially conscious. We decided to look for another apartment and found a beautiful flat on Jackson Street, half a block from my old Sacred Heart School.

But the rent was more than my mother could afford with the money Daddy was sending. She had given up her dressmaking when we took the trip to Mexico, and it would take time to reestablish her clientele. I had taken a leave of absence from college because I had come down with a terrible flu. I proposed not returning and looking for a job. My mother agreed; after all it was because of my beloved Russell that we had to move. I might as well contribute to the change.

The move was easy, my mother had sold some of the furniture in storage that wouldn't fit into our small apartment on Pine Street. What was left seemed lost in our new elegant flat. Not an apartment this time, a true flat with a separate entrance, not apartment doors all down a long hall. Mama planned to buy new furniture—on credit of course. This would be mine, when, in the far future, I married. Once settled, I started looking for a job.

It was difficult to land one with no experience. But finally Butler Brothers Wholesale Distributors took me on as a file clerk. I did know the alphabet. This lasted about six months, until the export department where I was employed shut down because of the war. Again to hunt, and this time I landed an exciting job with Four Roses Distilleries. I now had experience and was put in charge of the Federal Tax records. I was surprised at what percent of the price of a bottle goes to the Treasury.

1941 AT JACKSON STREET

As Christmas approached life seemed to be going smoothly, success in my job, fairly good relations between Russell and my mother, and a residence he actually admired.

It was my last happy time with Mama till several years later. We were worried of course about the war with Japan. Two or three times a week we heard air raid warning sirens. Out would go the lights; carrying a shaded flashlight, we drew the black curtains over the windows. Then we could have a little light; maybe one lamp in a room.

Very often Russell, who lived 6 blocks away with his Aunt Marie, would rush over and stay till the all clear siren sounded. One cold evening, my mother made Hot Toddys, and we sipped them and wondered if this would be *it*, the Japanese reaching our shores, by plane or ship. They did reach Santa Barbara in a small submarine, and let off a small barrage from some weapon that didn't do any harm. But that incident was enough to make us think it was possible they would reach us.

But actually all was not cozy and friendly in my mother's attitude toward Russell. First there were the arguments about Sundays. It was fine with her for me to be invited out on Saturday night, or even an occasional date on weekdays for a movie or dinner out or at his Aunt Marie's apartment. But Sundays were sacred to my mother. It was a family day, church, a nice lunch, and stay home, maybe have some company. Russell was welcome to come, but he told me he was bored just "sitting around." So he seldom joined us.

One time however, I had the courage to accept an invitation on a Sunday to join his parents, who lived in Marin County. They owned a small boat, which they kept in Tiburon, the charming little town on the Marin County seashore. My mother was furious at my going, "Leaving your mother and your brother on a Sunday." But for the first time in my life I stood up to her, and went off for the day with Russell's family. I enjoyed myself, but deep down felt guilty. Worse was yet to come -- the Easter incident!

Going off on Sunday, not being with my mother was bad enough, but to dare go with Russell, not my family to Easter Mass, that was unforgivable. Why did I do such a thing?

Russell was supposed to be Catholic, but had been lax about

going to Sunday Mass. In those days according to the Catholic Church, it was a hell fire sort of sin to miss Sunday Mass. I feared my beloved would go to the bad place if he didn't obey the rules. He said Mass was boring, all in Latin, BUT he would go to Easter Sunday Mass, and promise to continue attending on Sundays, if I would go with him. I promised I would, but when I told mama, she was furious. She and I shared a bedroom, and all that night she kept at me for my disloyalty to my family, for my wanting to be with that man on Easter Sunday. Then to my shock she burst out with "All you want is that thing stuck in you." I cried, and tried to make her see that I wanted to stop Russell from being in a state of Mortal Sin.

However, in spite of the terrible night, I got up early and was waiting out in front for Russell. I should have been relieved to be saving his soul, but the upset of the night before, and I guess guilt at having opposed my mother, caused me to faint during the Mass. I recovered in time to receive communion with my fiancée.

Very soon after this disturbing event, a letter arrived from my father. This letter changed all our lives.

DIVORCE

The letter was from Arthur, who had been away in Guatemala, now thirteen years. In his letters he had always said, "I hope to be with you for Christmas." But close to that time he would write, "Darling, I just can't make it for Christmas, not only because of lack of funds, but because several potential accounts look promising for early next year."

Then in 1940-41 he often wrote "I like it here, I will try to visit

you soon, but I don't want to permanently live in United States."
Adela did not take him seriously. She just ignored his words and
kept hoping he would return permanently.

But this letter, dated February 4, 1942 was different. It
commenced with financial details, when her next check might be
expected, etc. But paragraph two read:

*"I would like to confirm what I have told you in former letters;
that I do not intend to go to United States to live, definitely, at all. I
like Guatemala very much and at my age making changes is out of
the question, especially without considerable capital.*

*You have always said that you would not come to Guatemala
to live, that you prefer to live in the United States, instead of being
at my side in a place where I can make my living.*

*Thirteen years of separation have passed, and I have made roots
that are impossible to pull out. I have made deep friendships, both
men and women. Furthermore, my employees are like a family to
me. Leaving all this is impossible; there is no way we could again
form a conjugal union. In practice we have been as if divorced for
thirteen years; all that is needed is legalization."*

Once he had delivered the bombshell, he ended the letter with
matter of fact comments on my mother's unhappiness about my
engagement to Russell. She felt that Russell didn't seem to have a
good financial future, and furthermore he was inattentive to the
family, just wanted to take Mary off on trips to the seaside with
his family. He sympathized but added that love was a sickness that
was hard to combat.

Disbelief was my mother's, Malcolm's and my first reaction.

Mama seemed numb; "He must be mentally sick," was all she could say.

At first a trip to Guatemala seemed financially impossible. Then a second event here wiped the shock and worry from our minds.

Russell and I told my mother we wanted to get married that next June. He had lost his job in his father's grain export firm, which had closed because of the war. But two months later, Russell did get a job with Del Monte Foods, in the testing department. The salary was such that he could afford to get married.

My mother went to pieces. She couldn't stop crying, and locked herself in a dark room. Malcolm begged me to tell her we would wait. I was helpless and gave in. So for four months things calmed down. I don't know what subsequent letters from my father said. I only have a copy of his last letter written on June 12,1942. Here he was no longer polite. He demanded Adela not make trouble, just consent to the divorce. It would just be a waste of money to contest it, and he would get the divorce in the end.

We all, Malcolm, Russell, and I decided the only thing to do was for my mother to go to Guatemala. Somehow we got together enough money to buy her new clothes and the ticket to Guatemala. Russell contributed $300.

The Adela we put on the plane for Guatemala looked gorgeous. She had lost weight, her still dark brown hair was done up in a modern coiffure. I was absolutely sure she would save her marriage. This was June 20, 1942.

The next day I was at work at my Four Roses office. Janice

the switchboard operator said "Mary, Russell is on the phone for you."

"Mary," Russell's voice sounded urgent. "I am at the Coast Guard recruiting office. We have been engaged two years. Your mother will never give her consent! I will join up, unless you say you will marry me right away."

I immediately pictured his being killed, my losing him forever. Now that I was sure my mother would be reunited with my father, I said "yes!"

I started to cry, uncontrollably. Lucky the two bosses and all the salesmen were out. All three girls, Janice and the two secretaries, Shirley and Margy came rushing to my desk,

"What's the matter, honey?"

"Russell wants us to get married, or he will go into the Merchant Marine. We have been engaged 2 years, but as I have told you, my mother wants us to wait until the war is over."

"You silly goose," and putting her arms around me Shirley continued, "You just have to marry Russell. The company will give you as a wedding present, a phone call to Reno to make arrangements." Long distance phone calls in 1942 were still precious and rare enough to have "wedding gift" status.

So it was that a wedding was arranged at Our Lady of Snows in Reno, for June 24th. The next two days were frantic. Russell's parents were happy for us, but apprehensive about my mother.

They decided Aunt Marie, Mrs. Jones, and Gordon, Russell's brother would go with us.

Gone was my dream of a lovely wedding gown, but at least I wanted a virginal white suit. No such thing that season in San Francisco. A nice little blue linen one was my compromise. At least I was able to find a white hat!

This is my mother's story, so I will just say that we had a nice ceremony at the little old fashioned church in Reno. Our Lady of the Snows was no cathedral, but it suited the circumstances. We had a wonderful honeymoon at Carmel. I was sure my mother would forgive me. I was so happy. When we returned a week later, I went back to the boarding house. We had to keep our marriage secret until I told my mother.

Malcolm had gone to Los Angeles with Mother, where she was to catch her plane for Guatemala. When he returned, he was not surprised at my elopement. However, he made me promise to hold off telling mother till we knew how things were going in Guatemala.

In her first letter to us, mother said she had not seen Arthur; he had refused a meeting. That did not look good. Her second letter confirmed our fears.

Dear Mary and Malcolm:

Yesterday I was finally able to get into your Daddy Arthur's place.

I sat there in his room, so tidy, except for little notes pasted all over the desk. I wished he would come, the family said they would make him come. I kept saying to myself "He loved me, he loves me. Oh what do I know?" I kept repeating these words, and trying not to cry any more. Then I thought "Maybe he will kill me. No he loves

*me, he wrote it so many times. Please Arthur come; love me again.'
Then the door burst open; he stood there-- a white haired, cold,
statue of fury.*

*"Adela, have you no dignity? Why did you have to come, to force
this on me? It is over, as I said in my letter, we have been divorced
for more than 10 years to all extents and purposes."*

For a moment I just sat there thinking of THAT letter.

*Could I ever forget that letter, years of love letters that said, "I
will return soon, I miss you all so" Then that bomb shell. I looked at
my angry husband and finally I spoke to him,*

*"All I could think was to get to you as soon as possible. I was sure
you had gone crazy and needed help." Then I added, "What about
all your love letters until that last one asking for divorce?"*

*He replied, "El papel aquanta mucho!" "Paper can take on a
lot."*

*Then Arthur, your Daddy stormed out of the room. All I could
do was go back to your aunt Mary's house and go on crying.*

I will write again tomorrow. Love Mamita

I felt terrible. How could I tell her I was married? A whole
month went by, while I hoped somehow my parents would reunite.
But world events, Hitler invading Poland, the German Blitz over
Europe and then England, Hitler's invasion of Russia, and finally
our entering the war completely after Pearl Harbor, these events
finally personally affected our lives.

The draft reached more and more young men. Russell had tried
to join the Navy, but had been rejected because his eyesight was

terrible without glasses. Nevertheless, with the need for ever more manpower, the draft caught up with him. As long as he had to go, Russell had hoped to be sent overseas, but instead he landed at Benicia, California. It was a munitions depot.

Meanwhile down in Guatemala, Adela and Arthur struggled over the divorce–Arthur insisting, Adela refusing. Then Roosevelt lowered the draft age to18. Malcolm was 18. When he wrote Mama, that he soon would be in, that did it for her. She gave up and consented to the divorce.

Adela dressed all in red for the "ceremony." Red suit, red hat, red shoes; and the reddest lipstick she could find. She looked straight ahead all during the short hearing; crying would be for later. She held out a steady hand, fingernails painted bright red, to receive the paper that ended her marriage.

For more than a week we received no letters until finally one from Aunt Ruth arrived. "Adela is too upset to write." Then Ruth proceeded to give details of the whole sad affair. Her cousin would stay a few days until arrangements were made for her return to United States.

Now I had to tell mother that we were married. I wrote Mama a letter just saying that we had gotten married–no date. She never knew that a whole month had passed.

I wrote a second letter to Aunt Ruth, asking her to give mama my letter at whatever time seemed best to Ruth. Years later Ruth told me it was the most painful thing she ever had to do. If my mother went to pieces when we simply told her we wanted to get married in June, you can imagine the scene when she read my letter. But I wasn't there!

I saw my mother once when she got back. I went to Rosita Berheim's apartment, where my mother was staying until the Jackson Street apartment she had sublet was vacated. We might as well have been strangers. Adela greeted me with a cold "Hello Mrs. Jones."

It was a short and miserable visit, a visit that ended when I tried to hug her, and she coldly turned away and walked into another room. I let myself out, and for six months suffered her rejection. I would phone every day; mama would hang up.

After six months I received a letter from her, addressed to Mary Nicol Jones. It ended the rift.

CHAPTER IX -
RIFT AND RECONCILIATION

Dear Mary:

As you no doubt know, Malcolm is now stationed in Tyler Texas. If you would take a trip there with me, I would forgive you. Let me know what you and the Joneses decide. I am sure you would need their permission.

Adela.

We all talked it over. Mrs. Jones especially felt it was so sad that my mother and I were estranged. Russell said that as long as he was stuck in Benicia and got home so seldom, it was a good idea. So I phoned my mother, this time she answered.

It was decided that we would go by Greyhound bus. Flying was too expensive. We planned to stop overnight on the way, but as it turned out, we went straight to Tyler, sleeping on the bus for three nights. It was quite an adventure for me but for my mother it was terribly wearing. Only the thought of seeing her beloved Malcolm kept her going.

The difficult trip seemed worthwhile when we arrived at the charming, typically Southern town of Tyler. Malcolm had found us a little house, walking distance from his Air Corps barracks. He was able to visit almost every evening as his training to be the radioman on a B 24 was all in the daytime. There were parties at the USO, an invitation to tea at a real Southern Mansion, and a taste of hospitality as only Southerners can achieve.

The only problem was that Malcolm did not spend 100% of his free time with us. He had met a beautiful girl named Sally, and at times wanted to be with her instead of Mama and sister.

One evening when my mother made a terrible fuss and insisted Malcolm spend the evening with us instead of Sally, he whispered to me, when Mama was out of the room, "Mary, if I don't come back don't mourn me." Oh, words that would haunt me for years!

But mostly, things were pleasant, that is until a letter from Russell arrived. He had a foot injury and received a medical discharge. He must do war work, but he was now free and wanted me to come home immediately.

Of course I wanted nothing else, but my mother didn't see why. I couldn't just stay till Malcolm graduated and was assigned his new duties. I proposed going home alone. Impossible! Just then I caught a streptococcus infection, and was terribly sick. Then a second letter from Russell arrived. *"Come home now, or else!"* High fever and all, I got out of bed and started packing. My mother knew there must have been something in his letter to cause my determination to return home.

She found the letter and read it. For years she would not forgive Russell and she was impotent against my resolve to leave Tyler immediately.

We loaded our luggage on a Greyhound bus, but only went as far as Dallas. I was so sick that mama was afraid I wouldn't make it. She had a cousin in Dallas. Here the family saw to it that I had medical attention before we continued our trip. Just two days later, all full of drugs feeling like a Zombie, I traveled back to San Francisco.

. Russell was sorry that I was so sick but felt it was right that I should have come back now that he was out of the army.

A couple of weeks later, my mother wanted me to come and write some letters for her. She didn't trust her spelling in English, having been educated in German and Spanish. So I always did her English correspondence. I said I would come, but then the Joneses wanted Russell and me to go to Sausalito to see a little house that was for rent. Since my return we had been staying with Aunt Marie, but the family felt we should have our own place.

I insisted that before we go across the Golden Gate Bridge to Sausalito, we stop at my mother's apartment to tell her I couldn't do her letters that day. The Joneses stayed in the car while I went to tell Mama that I would help her another day. In a fury she, grabbed me by the hair and threw me down. Just then Russell came to see what was delaying me. He grabbed his mother-in-law and flung her into a large chair. "Let's get out of here!"

Upset as I was, we proceeded to Sausalito and rented a charming little house called "La Casita." I tried to phone Mama when we got back to San Francisco. She hung up. Daily I phoned, even after we were established in our little Sausalito house. Always she hung up.

I was afraid to go to her apartment, so was unaware of the miserable time she was having trying to live on the $50.00 a month alimony she had been awarded in the divorce. Later I learned she had been working in defense plants. But she was fired from job after job, always because she couldn't stop crying. Adela was crushed after all the years of love letters, of being faithful to my father. The divorce was a blow from which she just couldn't recover. She had devoted her whole life to a belief that had been false. Furthermore I, betrayed her by marrying when Russell and I had promised to wait.

My mother Adela's only consolation was that Malcolm had received his Air Corps Radio Operator certificate in Tyler; he was coming west, to be stationed at Mather Field in Marin County, across the Golden Gate bridge.

There was further training, mainly in connection with actual flight. On his frequent leaves, Malcolm could visit me in Sausalito. Of course, he went as often as possible to see Mother. She had been able to finally stop crying and being fired, and had earned enough to rent a small apartment on California Street.

Malcolm would plead with her to forgive me. "Russell isn't so bad," he would say. "He has a good job now, and he is good to Mary." But it was no use, all Adela would say to her son was, "She betrayed me when I trusted her."

On another visit Malcolm was very excited. "Mama, they have finally assigned us a plane and formed a crew. There are four officers, five gunners, and me the radioman." He was bitter about being made a Sergeant, not an officer. The fourth gunner was an officer and Malcolm felt Radioman was more important. The army Air Corps had its own ideas.

But Malcolm liked the men. They would be together for as long as the war lasted. As her son sat there in Mama's cozy living room, Malcolm continued telling her about the crew. "There is one sad thing, though. Two of the officers' wives have come west to be with their husbands. They would so like to be together for a last Christmas. The wives are now in a motel." Mama had an idea.

"There is a vacant apartment here in this building. I will ask the landlord if he would rent it for a short time to the two couples. It would be a patriotic act to give these departing soldiers one last joy. Typical of my mother, she not only persuaded the landlord to rent the vacant apartment but phoned various friends who would lend enough furniture to make the two couples comfortable. Adela's friends came up with beds a large table, some chairs and even a little radio. The two couples were able to be together at Christmas and for eight more days. On the ninth day the crew flew off to the South Pacific, where the war was at its fiercest.

* * * * * *

Now that Malcolm was gone my mother finally realized that the war work was impossible, that she must find some other way to support herself. Just then a friend of hers, Mrs. Oyos decided to retire from managing her large boarding house. She had put the house on the market, for $6,000, and was asking only $1000 down.

Adela asked her friend Dorothy Thomas to write her a letter to Mr. Jones, asking him to give her the thousand she needed to buy that house. This way she could support herself. The trouble was, however, that she put her request in such a way that made that amount the price of forgiving the Jones family for having allowed, in fact helped in our marrying, without her knowledge or consent. They had ruined her life. My mother felt that had I not married, I might have been able to go to Guatemala and somehow save her marriage. The least the Joneses could do was help her make a new life. She needed to support herself, to support herself in dignity.

Mr. Jones was furious. The whole family rushed over to our little house in Sausalito. Now I had their fury added to my mother's. Why didn't I plead with Mr. Jones to give her the money. He frightened me. Furthermore, Miss Brewer, Russell's aunt did go to see the house. She declared it was too expensive, and furthermore was too close to the "negro" district.

I had to tell my mother that Mr. Jones had refused to lend or give her the thousand. However, I said I would get a job and help her buy that house. Russell agreed to our moving to San Francisco. However, even before we made the change, I wrote several letters to advertising companies. The jist of the letter,

"I was bitten by the ad bug when I was advertising manager for a small campus paper. I would like to make advertising my career."

While awaiting the result of my letters we moved to San Francisco to nice top floor apartment on Washington Street, almost Nob Hill.

About ten encouraging letters came in answer. After several interviews, I was employed as assistant office manager by a publishers' representative, Duncan Scott.

But I failed miserably. The job was way over my head, seeing I had no office skills. So I enrolled in a secretarial school for which Russell paid the tuition. It was a good move, but again this is my mother's story. I will just say that long before I finished the secretarial course, Adela received a letter from a friend in San Salvador that would again change her life.

CHAPTER TEN -
OFFICER'S CLUB

The letter that came to Adela from San Salvador started a new, a happy chapter in my mother's life.

Sarita Pinto and Adelita had been girlhood friends in Nicaragua. Sarita had married a journalist from San Salvador, where the couple had lived an interesting and productive life. Jorge Pinto was a liberal journalist, dangerous in that country where the landed families literally ruled. Jorge once too often criticized their social injustices–the shot meant for his heart missed, but dangerously wounded his leg

In her letter to my mother Sarita said that they had arranged for a highly thought of surgeon in San Francisco to operate his wounded leg, hoping to save it. She asked her friend Adelita to look for a house, a rental, in San Francisco, where he could convalesce.

They would be arriving with their little son Jorjito and Jorge Pinto's nurse, Sylvia in two weeks.

During those two weeks Adelita must have seen a dozen houses. Then she was shown a three-story house, on the 2300 block of Broadway. It stood atop a steep Pacific Heights hill. The house was three stories high, with a spacious basement. Its brown shingle exterior and marble entrance steps made it very San Francisco. Entering by the carved front door, and stepping across the parquet hard wood entrance hall, past the wide red–carpeted stairs was the spacious parlor. Looking through huge beveled glass windows was a view of San Francisco Bay from the Golden Gate to Alcatraz Island.

Adela persuaded the real estate agent to hold it till the Pintos arrived. A week later, as soon as Jorge Pinto was installed in the hospital, and his family at the Fairmont Hotel, Adelita arranged for the Mrs. Pinto to see the Broadway House. Sarita was enchanted, but felt it was too big. Then the two ladies came up with a solution. That solution was finally to change my mother's life for good.

Adelita had told Sarita that she had tried to buy a house where she could rent rooms and support herself in decency. Her daughter's in-laws had refused to help, and her dream seemed hopeless. After learning this, Sarita proposed that she and her family take the bottom floor and a couple of rooms upstairs for the nurse and the little boy. Adelita could rent the rest of the rooms. When Jorge recovered, and they returned to San Salvador, Adelita could have the entire house. Sarita offered to lend her friend the money to furnish the Broadway house.

For two weeks Adela lived at Auction Houses, buying and

buying and buying. A friend of hers, who saw her bidding without stop, came up to her "Adela, do you know what you are doing?" My mother laughed and explained that she was furnishing a 12-room house. She did not go into the details, just said it was a business project. Her friend left her greatly relieved.

Finally all was ready and the Pintos, including Jorge who could now commence his long recovery moved in. All that remained was my mother's part, renting the remaining rooms. She had in the past, during the worst of the depression rented part of our apartment to girls. But this time she thought of renting only to officers in the U.S. military. She figured that if there were trouble with a tenant, she could contact his outfit and report any misbehavior. So it was that Adela's Officers Club was born.

Little by little the vacant rooms were rented. One uniformed young man after another moved in- Army, Navy, Marine, all officers. Not once did Adela have to call headquarters, they were all gentlemen.

Pinto enjoyed visits from the young men, and their tales of war experiences; several of the boys were on R & R (rest and recreation) leave. Pinto matched their stories with wild tales of narrow escapes the journalist had experienced before the last unhappy adventure.

After eight months, Jorge Pinto was sufficiently well to return to San Salvador. There had been a change of government, he felt relatively safe returning to his country and to the work he loved. So the house now became entirely mother's with the young military men, each one of whom she grew to love. Their regard for her became terribly important in the next few months, the months nearing Christmas.

* * * * * *

Russell and I were still in the wonderful little apartment on Nob Hill. One late afternoon I was cooking dinner when the phone rang. In case it was a long call, I turned off the stove, never to use it again.

MALCOLM

It was my mother, "Mary, come over immediately. Malcolm's plane has been lost."

"Oh mama, it can't be; the war is over. We'll be right over."

I shoved the food into the frig, we grabbed coats and piled into the car downstairs in front of the apartment. All the way to Broadway Russell kept reassuring me. "Mary, they are all confused, the government doesn't know its right hand from its left. You'll see it is a mistake."

We parked right in front of the house. I had a key so we let ourselves in and walked into the living room. There through the huge beveled windows I could see white caps on the bay, and could feel the November chill in the air. Not even the fragrant Pinewood burning in the fireplace could dispel the gloom.

I hugged and kissed my mother, and murmured, "It will be alright mama."

Russell added, "Yes, Mrs. Nicol, I am sure it is a mistake, they don't know what they are doing there in Washington. How did you hear anyway?"

Mama pointed to a young Air Corps man, Paul, one of the original crew members; from him we got the story.

The original crew did not stay together after Japan surrendered. Paul went ahead to Guam on a plane that had one space. They had drawn lots as to who would get that seat and had decided to meet in Guam when the rest of the crew, on their original B 24 made the three hour trip from the Philippines to Guam. But two days later, when the crew did not meet Paul at the designated place, he checked with headquarters and was told the plane never did arrive, though Malcolm had radioed they were on the way. Search parties had been dispatched immediately. The weather was perfect, but the search planes could find no wreckage."

"I thought you knew" Paul kept repeating. He had come merely to give condolences; little did he know he would be the messenger of this terrible news.

As our conversation continued, I suddenly recalled how on V.J. day my mother had not joined us in our celebrating; instead she had cried and cried, saying, "He's not home yet." Now that premonition seemed plausible; I shivered and thought, "He must be found."

As the officers living at Broadway came in that evening, they heard what had happened. Besides genuine sympathy, those with connections in Washington D.C. immediately got to work with telegrams inquiring about that plane.

We never did find out why my mother had not been notified; there were merely two telegrams which came in answer to the officer's inquiries. The first said, "Regret to inform you...son reported missing." Six months later, the second telegram, the official "presumed dead" arrived. What months of anguish those two pieces of paper represent.

The death of a loved one is hard to take, but aided by belief in a hereafter, it is bearable. After all, one finally reasons, when the first waves of misery have passed, that the loved one is now safe, having arrived where we are all hopefully headed. But with us there was always hope that he had survived. With that hope, we also felt the horror of what Malcolm and the other members of the crew might be experiencing.

Besides the information obtained by the officers, my mother heard from the family of the flight engineer on Malcolm's plane. The officer's father, Mr. Carter had powerful connections in Washington D.C. Our frequent correspondence, and phone conversations with him assured us that everything that money and power could do was being done to find that lost plane. We all needed to know for sure whether or not our boys were alive or dead.

When two months had passed, one of the officers took me aside. He told me there was really no hope. But he advised me, " Say nothing to Adela." Most of the officers addressed my mother as Mrs. Nicol, but Lt. Anderson was like a relative, very close to my mother. He continued, "Your mother will gradually come to know that there is no hope, but she must be allowed to realize at her own pace.

So it was, slowly, slowly as the months passed hope faded. Then just as the San Francisco summer fog was covering the city each morning hope was revived by a rumor.

Mr. Carter heard that the plane had landed on a Russian island named Aidan. Where he heard the rumor, I don't know. Hoping to get more information, I called the Russian consulate, which was still in San Francisco. I got the same run-—around we grew so used to during the subsequent cold war. After talking to three heavily accented voices, I came away with no information, neither das nor niet. I gave up. A navy friend of mine assured me it was but a rumor; Russians had no islands close to that location.

Meanwhile Russell had given up our apartment on Nob Hill, and had moved in with his parents, just half a block away. He kept hoping we could resume our normal life. However, though I had always been torn between my mother and Russell, this time there was no choice. This wounded human being, my mother, had to have me. I felt at first that I was literally holding her sanity in my own two hands. I slept in her bedroom, even when Russell finally accepted his mother-in-laws' offer of a room on the lower floor. It took me two weeks before I could leave mother and join Russell at night, in our room.

The next four months were not all gloom but there was no love lost between Russell and my mother. However, they both behaved like civilized people. Only when my mother had me alone, when we were working together making or changing beds, or preparing the coffee in a thermos and a Danish Pastry that we left at each door every Saturday night, would she go on with her carping about Russell. He would never become a millionaire. I would retort that he worked hard, was increasingly successful as a flour salesman. But that was not good enough!

But life has to have some fun!. I would organize picnics in the back yard, inviting the young officers to join us. We drank beer out of quart bottles, and almost could forget the horrible war.

All during those last four months, Russell not only did his day job, but at night would transport sacks of sugar from one baker, who had too much, to other bakers who did not have enough "war coupons" to buy the sugar they needed. Black market? Hmmm, it made good money, and filled a need for some of his customers.

Of course I did not dare tell my mother why he was out most nights. She began to wonder if our marriage might be in trouble.

I was pleased and surprised when she suggested that perhaps we should leave and buy a house. Russell of course, jumped at the suggestion, and that weekend we went to Sausalito house hunting. He had made plenty of money from his night work for a healthy down payment.

On our second weekend of hunting we found a wonderful little house, with a large Rose garden. It was in what was called "Hurricane Gulch," but had a view of the bay. We were almost ready to move in, negotiations were underway when a real estate friend of my mother's told her of a three unit apartment building, near our little house. Adela put down what money she had saved from Broadway rents. But she found her down payment was not enough. Her payments would have been too high. Then the Joneses came back into the picture, this time in a good way!

Aunt Marie thought the apartments would be a good investment for Russell. She offered to lend him enough money to repay my mother for the down payment she had made. Aunt Marie added enough to the loan to make his mortgage payments affordable. Furthermore, she felt the little house we had purchased was too humble, not a good investment. So we moved in just long enough to sell it, even made a profit.

ADELA'S REAL ESTATE ADVENTURES

Before we had even moved out of the little house and into one of the apartments in our new dwelling, the government insurance check for Malcolm arrived. My mother had barely had time to deposit the money, full wartime insurance, when she received a frantic call from Uncle Jack. He was about to lose his house for unpaid taxes.

Uncle Jack was actually my father's Uncle. It was his house to which we used to walk when we were staying at the Schuler's those three summers. Uncle Jack, John Malcolm Nicol, was a self educated Engineer. He had built the house almost by himself. He and his wife Susan had escaped to Marin County when their flat in San Francisco was totally destroyed in the 1906 San Francisco earthquake. They had camped on the lot they owned in Mill Valley until Uncle Jack was able to erect a proper house. He had lived there forty years, earning a living by engineering jobs in various mines in Central America. Aunt Sue had become an invalid and lingered on for years till she died. There were terrible medical and care expenses, so he had not been able to save for his old age.

. As years went by taxes were increased, he could no longer work at the demanding mining jobs he had undertaken. So month by month he fell further behind.

"Could you help me Adela? I will die if I lose my house, and anyway if I sell it where would I go?"

Adela just couldn't let $10,000 just sit there and let an old man lose the home he had built. So she paid the back taxes, and proceeded to change ownership. Once all papers were signed, my mother suggested to Uncle Jack that he rent a room. She thought the rent would be a little income for Uncle Jack, and maybe the tenant would be good company.

. The tenant, Elizabeth McBride turned out to be a witch of a woman. She yelled at the old man, complained about the lack of heat, and was always late with her rent.

Uncle Jack phoned my mother almost daily, complaining about his tenant, and each time telling of one more repair that was needed on the house. At first his niece Adela fixed whatever was broken, or worn out. Finally, she had to tell him, "Uncle Jack, I am fast going through the insurance money, I just can't keep it up." She consulted with Russell and me. Together we came up with a solution. She would sell the house and install Uncle Jack in a small apartment in our three unit complex. She would pay the rent to us, and in turn I would see that Uncle Jack was cared for. His food and small expenses were taken care of by a little annuity a nephew had established long ago. Not enough to have saved his house, but adequate for his present needs.

Adela sold the house through the same real estate friend who had suggested she buy our three unit apartment house. He had gotten a very good price for Uncle Jack's house and suggested she immediately invest in a pair of flats he had for sale in the Marina. Tax wise it was a good deal so my mother told him yes.

Two years passed before major changes came into both of our lives. The Broadway house changed from an officer's club, to a young man's club. The young men who rented there were well to do bachelors, not yet settled enough in life to have their own apartment or start a family. Their names were often on the Society page, or in the business section when they entered executive ranks.

Adela decided she would serve meals now that she had tenants with regular hours. The meals were formal, Adela seated at the head of a well appointed table, a maid ready to come right in when the tiny bell tinkled. As one young man after another fell in love, courted and finally married, Adela was always invited to the wedding.

Meanwhile in Sausalito life was good for Russell and me. We wanted a child but somehow I never seemed to get pregnant. But life was so much fun, and work on my garden so satisfying that I really didn't mind. Uncle Jack was a slight problem; he would annoy Russell with phone calls late at night when he thought he was having an asthma attack. Poor old man was just lonesome.

When one of our tenants moved out of our best apartment, we decided to redo it and get more rent. That summer was spent overseeing a fireplace being built, a skylight in one of the dark rooms, and a completely redone kitchen. When it was all completed we were able to ask a good rent. I was able to afford a cleaning woman and a gardener for the half acre surrounding the apartments.

Then came a blow! The O P A, a government rental regulation agency sent us a letter. We were charging too much rent. It must be reduced. We were allowed to raise the old rent only $5 a month. We had spent $3,000 in the renovation and only allowed a measly $5.00. Russell decided we must sell. Furthermore, he was increasingly annoyed with Uncle Jack.

Meanwhile although my mother was only in her late 50's, she was feeling constantly tired, and having trouble with insomnia.

She would take a sleeping pill, but three hours later would be wide awake. She also worried about me; was it the right thing to sell our apartment house? She wondered what would become of Uncle Jack with our being gone.

The Uncle Jack problem was solved by Hugh Nicol, his nephew. Hugh was the son of uncle Jack's brother Henry. That family's history is another story. Suffice it to tell that Hugh lived with his widowed mother in Mill Valley. When my mother asked him if he would take Uncle Jack, Hugh enthusiastically said yes. We wont say what he thought of his decision when Uncle Jack became difficult. Anyway Russell was now free to sell the apartment house. It sold immediately for a slight profit. At the same time, my mother decided she would sell her flats. This time a very good profit. So the Nicol and Jones families were free for the next phase.

* * * * * * *

Archbishop Mitty of San Francisco was organizing a pilgrimage to Lourdes and Rome. With the money from her flats Adela decided she wanted to join that pilgrimage. She proposed I join her. I was reluctant to leave Russell, who had developed an ulcer due to the hectic pace of Real Estate. He had passed a brokers test and had joined his Aunt Marie in her successful but demanding business. Russell said to me, "Accept your mother's invitation. I probably will never be able to afford to take you to Europe."

So it was that Adela bought two first class tickets to the Pilgrimage. First we crossed the Atlantic on the Queen Mary, then on to Lourdes, France, Switzerland and Rome, Italy. In Italy an Italian charismatic monk finally brought peace to a still bereaved mother.

CHAPTER IX -
EUROPE

Six months after our return from this trip I found a copy of my Mother's journal written during the Pilgrimage to Europe. It was written all in Spanish.

Here is my translation, but all in her own words.

I was afraid our trip would be a disaster. As soon as we got off the plane, retrieved our luggage and had it loaded into a cab, we proceeded to look for a hotel. The travel agent had said it was not necessary to make hotel reservations. They felt a taxi driver would take us to a suitable one.

Our driver was eager to help, but the first four hotels he tried were full. Finally at the Belmont Plaza on Lexington and Ninth we were able to get a suite. The desk clerk promised us a single room for the next two days when we would board the Queen Mary. I was horrified at the price, but Mary danced all through the spacious rooms. "Too bad we can't have a party."

That would be the last thing I would want, I just wanted to lie down until time for dinner. In fact I told Mary to order room service.

She was too excited to rest, spent the time before our meal arrived looking through tourist information. But after dinner she insisted we go out, "Times Square on Broadway I just have to see." She thought everything about New York would be glamorous but was disappointed to see noisy hash joints, sloppy girls hanging onto sailors arms, junky piled up Army Surplus stores, and an ambling, gum chewing mob.

The next day Mary wanted to visit some people with whom she had corresponded, so I was able to rest. The last two days the only activities we did together were a double Decker bus tour of the city and an evening at Radio City to see the Rockettes.

When finally the day arrived we were to board the Queen Mary–my daughter told me to say "The Mary" like a seasoned traveler. I was glad to have rested those three days in New York, because the ship left port at five in the morning.

Mary reserved two chairs on deck, where we could watch the New York skyline, still lit up before dawn. When we were finally out to sea we went below to our cabin. I told Mary, "I am not moving from here for twenty four hours. You go ahead tomorrow morning and arrange for our table. Give the headwaiter a good tip and tell him we want an interesting companion. In the afternoon you have to do the paper work. I did all that when I was young, now it's your turn. Oh yes, as soon as you have arranged the dining room seating, be sure you reserve two deck chairs. I am having all my meals in here tomorrow. I just have to get my strength back. You wore me out in New York."

"Alright mama," she answered, and added "You did get rest in New York, but I guess even the little you did was too much."

The next day Mary followed all my instructions. She kept coming to the cabin to check on me. She seemed quite impressed with the table companion we had been assigned. Mr. Wright was a vice president of Ford Motor Company's Farming division. He was returning from an Agricultural survey of United States and Canada.

The next day I did get dressed and went to lunch with Mary. Mr. Wright was nice enough, but in the subsequent days of the five-day voyage, I became increasingly annoyed. He monopolized Mary's time. They had long talks about gardening. I always thought Mary worked much too hard on their garden in Sausalito. Good they had sold the apartment house. But most of all I was annoyed at those long walks around the deck, which ended by their standing on the prow of the ship, the wind almost blowing them down. She would come back all enthused, "Mama why don't you come with us next time." Foolish girl, she knows my legs and my knees hurt too much. She spent much too much time with that Englishman- dirty old fool."

When we reached Cherbourg we were transferred to land in tenders, we were all crowded onto hard wooden benches. However, I enjoyed the three hour train trip to Paris. I warned Mary, "You will be disappointed at first. I was the first time I saw Paris. It is dirty, crowded, not picture card perfect. But I predict Mary you will fall in love with Paris, I certainly did." I was right about both parts, the disappointment, then the growing fascination with this witch of a city. The carriage ride we took after our first dinner totally converted her. To me it brought a flood of memories of the time I spent in the Nicaraguan Embassy in 1912.

The next two days were spent seeing art galleries, Versailles, the Petit Trianon, and Notre Dame Cathedral, which was shockingly neglected, dirty, full of rude tourists and cold in spite of the hot weather.

The third day in Paris I was too exhausted, and let Mary go on by herself. When the tour guide asked about me, she told him "Ma mere est malade." That word Malade! I had been ill the first time I came and they all chattered Malade, Malade. Every time I come to France they say I am "bad". Malade sounds like the Spanish word Mala, which means bad.

Mother's journal just listed other cities we visited. Merely passing by them by train were Tours, Pointier, Bordeaux, Dax; and one day stops at Nice, Monaco, and Rappalo. For Lourdes she had written;

Lourdes was impressive, but I was tired, and overwhelmed by the hordes of people. I maneuvered it so that Mary did not go and bathe in the miraculous waters. I guess my faith is not that strong that I would let my dear child get into that freezing pool, where all sorts of sick people have been immersed. She was cross with me when I confessed she could have gone, but I think I did the right thing.

Then Rome! As far as I was concerned the trip was over. This is why I had come; it had been good. The highlight was the audience with Pope Pius Twelve. He spoke to each of us personally. He asked Mary if she was a student. When she replied that she was married, he said, "That is good too."

Little did we know that that evening, in the lobby of our hotel, The Quirinale we would hear something that would bring us a deep religious experience.

PADRE PIO THE MONK

One of the travelers told us about a monk, Padre Pio who lived in the mountains of San Giovani Rotondo, near Foggia. I was determined to see him. Perhaps he could bring me peace, tell me whether my son was still alive, or if he had died.

First Mary phoned the Jesuit Mother House to inquire about the monk. She was assured he was indeed a holy man; yes he did have the gift of seeing the holy souls. Mary then learned how to get to San Giovani–train to Foggia, and then a hired car to the town where Padre Pio's monastery was located.

The hotel helped us make arrangements, train, then a car that would meet us in Foggia. By the next day it was all settled and we taxied to the train station, tickets in hand. The train trip was beautiful, glimpses of the Adriatic as we veered east. We were to meet the driver at a restaurant, El Fornario on the main street of Foggia. The driver seemed to understand Mary's funny Italianized Spanish, and politely helped us into the back seat of his little Fiat.

We drove an hour and a half on a winding mountain road. Finally we arrived at a barren little town. "San Giovani Rotondo," announced the driver. We had wondered where we would stay but the driver immediately told us he knew of a nice pension and proceeded to take us there. The woman who showed us our room spoke not a word of English, but managed to convey to the Spanish-speaking signoras that there was an American priest in the house. Would we like to meet him? Would we! She would tell Padre De Lire to come to our room.

We hadn't spoken English, except to each other, for more than twelve hours. There were so many questions we wanted to ask about Padre Pio. How, when and where would one get to his convent? How would we be able to talk to him?

About half an hour later there was a knock at our door. We opened it to see a T-shirted, rugged looking American male. There was one place to sit, the straw mattress on one of the beds. We bid Father De Lire sit. He had been there several days. He told us he was the pastor of a parish in a tough neighborhood of Chicago. He had come on a badly needed vacation to Italy. Hearing of Padre Pio, he felt an over powering need to see him.

Father De Lire was no simple padre. He was a rugged American, a priest in a fast paced city. He had a Doctorate in Sociology from Notre Dame University. But when he spoke of Padre Pio, this man was awed. He had been to confession and had expected a scolding for not being a saint. But Padre Pio had instead encouraged him to become a better person, to continue doing as well as he had, which the monk judged was father's best. "De Lire, you are going to do better," the priest had told himself.

Then father told us much about Padre Pio. The monk's mass lasted two and a half hours because he so often went into ecstasy.

Atheistic Communism had swept over Italy; post war poverty made it attractive. Padre Pio had converted many Communists. A man would come to Padre Pio on a bet that he was tough and could resist the monk's persuasion. Most of the "tough" ones renounced Communism and Atheism and returned to the faith of their youth.

Many stories were told of Padre Pio's gifts of bi-location, of his cures of the sick, of his gifts of tongues. But most talked about was his stigmata. The monk usually kept his hands hidden; he wore mitts over them. His long robe hid his feet and the wound on the side. However during mass, especially when he stretched out his arms, one could see the stigmata. As mass was to commence at four in the morning, Father De Lire left us and we retired to our straw mattresses.

It was cold that next morning; San Giovani is high in the mountains. We thought we had dressed plainly, just cotton dresses and scarves over our heads. But we were stared at nevertheless. The chapel of the monastery, which stood at the top of a hill was large and had several altars. Other priests were saying mass as we arrived. We asked which was Padre Pio and were shown a side altar, where a bearded priest was just ascending the altar steps. There were no benches just a few chairs in the center of the chapel. We knelt on the bare floor near the altar where Padre Pio was saying mass. I didn't last long on my knees, took a chair and sat down. Mary tried to be noble, but paid by feeling faint and having to go outside.

When she returned, I had received communion from another priest. But she returned in time to see Padre Pio stretch out his arms in prayer. The stigmata was visible.

Oh God, not like that! I had imagined neat little holes in the center of his hands, like the pictures we see of Christ. But here the entire palm was covered with dried blood, fresh red blood oozed out of the center. Passion is not tidy. Mary received communion from Padre Pio, and as soon as his mass was finished we left for the pension. There we met father De Lire, who had arranged for us to see Padre Pio. Father Dominic, an American priest in the monastery heard my story and said he would see that I talked with Padre Pio. We were to meet him at an open passageway from the church to the monastery. Padre Pio passed there around noon, when he would go to the dining hall for his only meal of the day.

We went there way before noon and after half an hour the American monk came. When he saw Padre Pio approaching he held a quick conversation and pointed to us. Then the American monk beckoned for us to come. Padre Pio spoke to me in Italian, which I could almost understand. But Father Dominic translated and said " Padre sympathizes with you in your sorrow." I quickly asked "Is my son alive." All Padre Pio, the priest gifted by God with the power of seeing the holy souls, of knowing where each one was in the hereafter—he simply said that I must resign myself to God's will. All this way to hear what I already knew. But something had happened. I felt peace, life became tolerable again. A year later I received a letter from Padre's secretary, "My son was safe in heaven."

In planning this trip I had wondered if I might be foolish, spending money that I well might need in my old age. But the

Padre Pio experience, and the fact that I had completed Mary's education seemed to make it right. Even if Russell would never be able to give her the luxuries I had had in my youth and that I felt she deserved, she had had a taste of what I had wanted for her. But only God knows what is best. She is certainly a happy, outgoing young woman.

So ended the journal. As thanks to mama I wrote a detailed account of the trip. It was professionally typed and bound in a pink leather book. Parts were published later in a Catholic magazine.

The years after our trip, the last chapter of my mother's life maybe answers why the lady lies there with a lacy handkerchief over her face.

CHAPTER TWELVE
THE FINAL THIRTY YEARS

She was variously called Adelita, Adela, Mama, Mamita, Lita and even Moycia, the pet name my father used; these names tell of her life. Her life in Nicaragua, then in Germany, first in childhood and later as a young lady in Paris gowns. They tell of her life from marriage, children, overcoming ordeals; the 1929 depression, her divorce, Malcolm's death, and great disappointment in her daughter. But finally at least there was resignation and acceptance of me as I am.

The final chapter begins at the Broadway house, where mama's life had taken a better turn. But now she knew that she couldn't go on doing as much as before her trip. She told the young men she no longer would be serving meals. Her knees were beginning to pain whenever she stood or walked. But mama continued making the beds, helping the Japanese boy who cleaned twice a week and in general keeping up Broadway.

However, in 1952, when a lease expired, she gave notice and took an apartment at 2952 California Street. It overlooked Lafayette Park, its trees and lawns framing a mansion on the other side of the park. Two of her young men wanted to stay with Adela and rented two of the bedrooms.

Marty Hofheinz was a retired army captain. He stayed with my mother until he married two years later. Of course Adela was invited to the splendid wedding held at the San Francisco officers' club.

Bunny Wolfe was from an old San Francisco family. Wealth and its trappings did not impress him. Bunny, (I never did know his real first name,) dreamed of one world, with no war, with the goods of the world equally distributed. I asked him if that wasn't Communism. "No no, this is different, Communism imposes itself, the "One World" organization is based on fairness, without being sentimental. " I would say with love." Oh yes, Bunny worked at a regular job, had graduated from college after the war, but he spent all his spare time on his ideal of "One World." He stayed a year after Marty left. Again there was a lavish wedding, and Adela was invited and treated by the family as a second mama to their son.

My mother kept in touch with several of her young men by letter and phone. Among them was Dick Winslow who became a dentist and moved to Tennessee, his home state. Another Southerner was Bill who became a lawyer. But her closest "boys" were Albert, Nelius Charles Mimes and Francis Brown.

Charles lived in Memphis, Tennessee. His family had a large motel, which Charles learned to manage when he went back. His letters kept begging Adela to come for a visit. Finally he succeeded and my mama, already shaky on her legs, flew to Memphis, even had to change planes half way. I don't recall whether Charles sent her the ticket, probably; her finances were never enough to afford trips. I have a snapshot of her draped in a huge apron and feeding the chickens in the Mimes back yard. She was very proud that she had been a success with "country folk."

But her great pride–she felt she had a good deal of influence in their decisions–was Albert Nelius and Francis Brown. Albert became an Episcopalian minister, and Francis a Catholic priest. "I have a priest and a minister" Mama would say proudly. She had urged both young men to return home. "There you will find what you are meant to do with your lives.

In the years after our trip to Tyler, Texas there were many ups and downs in my relationship with my mother. The main complaint? I did not see her enough.

On my return from Europe, Russell rented an apartment in the Marina district of San Francisco. It was utterly devoid of charm. But after redoing the furniture, and plunging into a course in Theology, and relying on Russell's promise of moving to a more interesting place, I was content. The good part was that I had time to see mama every day. But a year later the "interesting place to live" that Russell had promised became a glamorous houseboat. It had been built for a rich New York girl who wanted to try an "unusual" way of life. However, she soon grew tired of the houseboat.

One weekend when we had come to Sausalito to see Russell's brother Gordon, who lived across the street from the Yacht Harbor, we spotted that houseboat and inquired about the "For rent" sign on the dock. The harbormaster said he was in charge of the rental.

Right there and then Russell paid a deposit after we had inspected the houseboat. It had a large living room with a metal fireplace, two small bedrooms and a tiny but efficient "galley."

No more daily visits with mama. There were parties on our "Boat;" parties and meetings at the Sausalito Womens'club up on the hill. I had rejoined after some year's absence. Then I finally realized my ambition to write. I became Yachting Editor for the local newspaper. Later I graduated to the Marin County Daily, where I was able to do feature articles in addition to my yachting column.

With all this activity, mama constantly complained that I did not see her often enough. She did have a life, several friends with whom she dined every Sunday at a different restaurant. But my weekly trips to San Francisco to meet her at St. Boniface church for mass and lunch afterwards were not enough. Mama looked so sad every time she took me to the Greyhound bus for my return to Sausalito.

But a trip I made to Mexico with Russell's Aunt Marie turned Mama's sadness to fury again.

REUNION WITH FATHER

All the nine years since the divorce I had not written or contacted my father. Mama had insisted I burn all his letters, weekly letters I received all during my childhood and on to the time of their divorce. But in 1951 Aunt Marie wanted to go to Tapachula, Mexico to see an old aunt with whom she had always corresponded ever since her parents had left Mexico when Aunt Marie was a child. Russell encouraged me to go with her to translate. Marie had almost totally lost her Spanish.

It was a lovely, interesting trip, but I need tell only of the last part.

Tapachula was only an hour's flight from Guatemala City. Aunt Marie asked me if I would like to go there and see the many relatives who lived there. My father was by then living in Mexico, so I didn't fear breaking the promise to mama never to see him again. So off we went and spent a wonderful week. We stayed in a hotel, but my relatives entertained us royally. Uncle Henry put a car and chauffer at our disposal. There were trips to lake Atitlan, a half days trip from the capital, Lake Amatitlan, up in the mountains. Then there were fabulous meals, some at home others in a restaurant.

Finally the entire family took us to the airport. Aunt Marie wanted to stop in Mexico, there were more relatives she wanted to meet in Mexico City.

So on our last day in Guatemala, we all walked across the tarmac to the plane. As I was beginning to go up the steps, Uncle Henry took me aside and said, "Your father is meeting you at the Mexico City airport!" There was nothing I could do but enter the plane and spend the next three hours suffering. Aunt Marie gently said to me "Mary, I guess you are having your own three hours agony. "

Arriving in Mexico, we left the plane and entered the waiting room. I immediately recognized my father, standing soldier straight, a handsome man with his shock of snow white hair. He slowly, hesitantly walked toward me; I opened my arms and we embraced. His first words were, "I was nervous at how you would greet me."

I did not want to meet Carmen his wife, but the children we saw many times, at our hotel, or meeting in a restaurant. In later years, my two sisters, Ivy and Lillie and brother Melvin became very close to me.

One incident stands out in my mind; it helped me understand the breakup of my parents.

Aunt Marie had been picked up by one of her relatives and I was alone in our hotel room with my father. He asked me "Would you consider reading the Christian Science Lesson with me now?" Little Catholic girl I hesitated a moment, breathed a quick prayer to the Holy Ghost then said yes Daddy I will.

He read the lesson for about five minutes then suddenly stopped.

He looked at me intensely and said, "Do you think that if your mother, Adelita, my wife had tried to understand, as you do, and not gotten into her violent tempers, that our marriage would have remained whole."

I nodded, "Yes."

Then he continued, "I was just as much at fault as she was."

Then he thoughtfully admitted, in answer to my question,

"Daddy, why didn't you ever come to see us?"

"Perhaps I left to escape. I feel it was wrong–I was weak in leaving the ship–even though it was sinking. Adelita needed help."

So then I said, "Guess the job that you forsook is left to me." He replied, "Yes, child, you are love."

* * * * * * *

After a wonderful farewell party with Aunt Marie's relatives, she and I packed up and flew back to San Francisco.

But upon my return to San Francisco, what did mama say about this turn of events, events that were thrust upon me?

I decided to face the music as soon as possible. Russell drove me to mama's apartment but said he would pick me up later. No "Lion's Den" for him!

Mama was furious that I had seen Arthur, spent time with him.

"You love your bad father as much as you love me. How Can you!"

Then she calmed down. She had an idea. "As long as you contacted the man, maybe you should write him a letter and ask him to increase my "allowance" Since closing the Broadway house I have been very short."

So I said I would send a letter right away. I quote Daddy's answering letter dated May 1953.

My Darling Chichi:

I have before me your last two letters. In the second one you ask me to endeavor to send Adelita, your mother a larger amount of *money each month. I have followed your suggestion and asked my partner in Guatemala to instruct Owens Illinois Glass Co. of Toledo to send her $150 monthly instead of $100 as heretofore. I trust that this will meet with my darling daughter's approval. Thank you darling for bringing it to my attention.*

In the next twenty years the $150 gradually became $250, even after Daddy died. Carmen his wife continued sending the checks until the Mexican Peso was hugely devalued and sending dollars was financially impossible. But by then mama had managed to receive another source of income.

Walter Walsh, a lawyer friend of ours had been able to arrange a Veterans Pension connected with her son's death. When she reached age 62, a small Social Security payment earned from her war work was added to the pension. It gave mama just enough to support her simple life style.

DANCING, WRITING, BABIES (?)

My own life was as always busy. Children's dancing classes, writing my yachting column and feature stories, finally giving up the classes in favor of increased writing.

.

My weekly trips to San Francisco to visit mama of course were a priority. Then there was always a wish, maybe vague, to have babies. Finally I did see a Gynecologist who felt I should have an operation.

So my vague wish became concrete when I arranged to have

a Laparoscopy. About three days before going into the hospital, I told Russell to make arrangements for his meals somewhere. I told my mother, and though she didn't approve, she offered to have me stay with her till I felt well enough to go home. Russell was amazed. "You always talked about it, I never thought you would actually do it."

Mama was disappointed that I only stayed a week. She blamed Russell, who would only visit me for half an hour at a time; he felt too cramped and bored just sitting there talking to us.

The next two years 1954 to 1956 brought no pregnancy, but a hectic life of teaching, writing, activities at the women's club, and finally a move from our houseboat to an apartment across Sausalito's Bridgeway to a one bedroom apartment, high up on the hill, surrounded by trees. We had decided on adoption; no agency would accept parents who lived on a houseboat.

Mama came frequently by bus, and in spite of her increasingly bad knees, slowly climbed the winding stairs to our apartment. I would always walk down to the station with her. One time she suddenly asked, "Mary, why do you want to adopt?"

"Because, mama, I don't want to go to hell." She understood, and had to agree we led rather selfish lives, were not giving of ourselves

What started me really trying to succeed in adoption, after we had been rejected by social Service and other agencies was a retreat I made with mama at Vallombrosa in Menlo Park. It was her birthday August 8th, 1954.

It was a "closed" retreat. One stays on the premises all three days. When there wasn't a talk and prayer, we sat under the huge Gingo tree, surrounded by blooming Azaleas, light pink to deep rose.

I sorted out the whirling things in my life. The writing bug had bitten me much more than dancing ever had. Frankly I have never had the physical strength nor the wind for dancing.

BUT BABIES! What about that? God knows I had tried. Those three days of retreat brought a certain order, the relaxation of putting things in God's hands. He would send the babies if and when it was right.

That next year I pursued BABIES in a business like manner. First I contacted a lawyer who specialized in "gray market" adoptions –direct contact between adoptive couple and expectant mother. Some young women who found themselves with an unwanted pregnancy wished to avoid the social work labyrinth, opted for a direct adoption through a lawyer.

But this did not work out for us. Russell only wanted a girl–boys are too noisy, and besides there are enough boys in our extended family.

So our lawyer suggested we try Canada. He inquired for us; there were plenty of Catholic babies available; we could choose boy or girl just as soon as we were approved by their social service.

He sent for the papers which we filled out, adding letters from friends and our priest saying we were a "Sunday observing, church going, kind hearted couple."

We gained a picture of rural Canada from the questions on the application.

HOW NEAR IS THE NEAREST TELEPHONE?

HOW CLOSE IS THE NEAREST RAILROADSTATION?

IS THERE A SCHOOL IN YOUR VICINITY?

These questions conjured up a picture of vast prairies and lonely farm houses. Canada at this time had only 15 million people, same as California, but with a larger area than all United States.

Two months later we were on our way to Canada, by car to British Columbia, then train to Edmonton.

This is my mother's story, and her relations with the child we adopted are a vital part of the story. We saw several children, but I will quote from my journal what I wrote when we finally chose.

Once again we were ushered into the living room of a foster family. This child did not choose to be "shown," she screamed, she stared resentfully when I tried to take her, and with great dignity pushed away a trinket I handed her. So the little tyke's foster mother picked her up and held her in her lap till the little two year old stopped crying. However the suspicious glare remained. I sat on the floor and just looked at her. Finally, she slithered off Mrs. Saunter's lap, and after staring for ten more minutes, crawled over to me and put her head on my breast. No coochy cooing here, just two human beings melted into one, my tears running freely on the hard little head under my chin. She stayed there, unmoving while the others talked. Finally, as if from a thousand miles away, I heard Russell say, This child gets my vote. What do you say, Mary?"

I turned to him, "Need you ask?" and that was it.

LORRETTA

Russell wanted our baby who was half French and half Ukrainian, to have a name we chose, instead of her birth name Monica Laroque. After much research for a Ukrainian name we chose Lorretta. Lorretto in Ukraine is said to be the town where the Blessed Virgin Mary lived in her later years.

As soon as we had made this decision and seen the judge and knew we really had a baby I sent my mother a telegram.

GRANMOTHER LITA

"HAVE A BEAUTIFUL TWO YEAR OLD GIRL NAMED LORRETTA. BE HOME WEEK AFTER NEXT. LOVE RUSSELL & MARY."

The next day we started home. First we took the train to British Columbia where we had left our car. Then a leisurely trip back to Sausalito. Lorrie was like a seasoned traveler, quietly looking out the window, pointing to a sheep scrambling up a mountain hill, "Cheval" horse, she pointed. She had a funny combination of baby French and the English learned during her two months in the Saunter's foster home. In fact the nickname we had for Lorrie soon after we had her was "sugaldie". She kept saying that word and pointing to her feet. Later I figured it was baby French for soulier.

When we got home we immediately went to a children's shoe store. The clerk was shocked at the terrible fit on the child's old shoes. "No wonder, as you told me she resisted walking." The clerk said shaking his head.

When she had been fitted into the proper little boots, we set her on the floor and at first hesitantly, then happily she marched across the floor Chuckling, "These shoes walk so nice."

The minute we were unpacked and settled we drove across the Golden Gate Bridge and on to 2965 California Street. I had phoned ahead, so mama was prepared to meet her grandchild. The door opened and immediately mama bent down and opened her arms.

Lorrie took one look and accepted this new person. There was always a special bond between them.

I saw mama much more often now. I quit teaching dancing, and greatly cut down on my newspaper work. In fact one time when I had put Lorrie down in the crib we had installed in our bedroom, she stood up and grabbed the picture of a boat about which I had written a feature article. She tore it and gleefully laughed at her mischief. Russell and I were standing at the door and he said "Oh Mary, maybe that is a sign." Sign or not the column and the newspaper no longer seemed important. Someone else could do it.

Six months passed before mama did any babysitting alone. But she came often to the new house we bought in Mill Valley and stayed overnight in a guest room we had off the living room. We needed more room, as we had decided Lorrie needed a sibling. It was impossible not to spoil her. But I did try to keep some privacy. I created a grownup's, candlelight atmosphere at dinner time.

Lorrie was to stay in her room while we dined.

However, my mother thought I was cruel by insisting that Lorrie stay in her own room when we ate dinner. One of those times when she was visiting us, Lorrie was slowly going up the stairs. She kept murmuring sadly, "Mommy Daddy having dinner, Lorrie bye bye."

So my mother had quickly finished her dinner and gone up to her grandchild's room. Lorrie quickly cleared a chair and happily said "Oh Lita, keep me company!" Lita was the name mama had decided Lorrie and a future child would use instead of Grandma; Lita from Adelita

Before telling of our second adoption and my mother's relations with both children I need to tell of a little trip we took that shows that Adela was a good sport and still as adventuresome as she had been.

LAS VEGAS

Before he grew almost blind and frail in his eighties, Russell was a great one for thinking of a fun thing to do on the spur of the moment. One late afternoon, he said "Wouldn't it be fun to drive to Las Vegas, start now and drive all night?" I felt it was crazy, but love adventure, so agreed. Then he said "Why don't you phone your mother, ask her if she would like to go; could she be ready in a couple of hours?" I jumped at the chance, and phoned mama. She only hesitated one second and said sure, I'll be ready by 6:30."

So it was we three piled into the car and drove to the city to pick up my mother. She was all ready, and sat in the back seat with Lorrie, laughingly she said "Russell, I didn't know you could be so crazy."

Lorrie soon fell asleep, as did I, but mama tells that she had to keep Russell awake. She would tap his shoulder if he looked as if he were nodding. Furthermore she kept talking to him. But we arrived safe at Las Vegas and checked into a motel. Guy Lombardo was playing at one of the casinos. His whole orchestra was booked into our same motel.

We stayed three days, and took turns with nights out. One time it was Russell and me, another time mama and I went to the Guy Lombardo show.

Lorrie slept in the big bed with my mother, and one night slipped out of the bed onto the floor. My mother panicked when she didn't feel her next to her, and fished down on the floor, praying Lorrie wouldn't wake up and cry, disturbing Russell. But all ended well, she got Lorrie back in bed without even waking her.

CONNIE

When we returned home the papers were in our mailbox confirming our acceptance for the adoption of a second little girl. We were going to leave Lorrie with the Seymours, who had a boy her age. However Lorrie had different ideas. She was so obnoxious during a trial run, that the Seymours rescinded their offer to keep her. So we all three drove all the way to Edmonton. At every stop Lorrie would ask "Where is my sister?" "Not yet Lorrie, we have to go where she is."

When we finally arrived at Edmonton we started our rounds with Lorrie in tow. I was so glad we had brought her, observing her with the children we visited made choice easier. In retrospect, I can imagine no other choice than our Connie. She is so much ours.

It is very difficult to know what a child is really like under the trying circumstances of being looked over. And this Connie of ours was anything but a simple little child. Beneath her submissive exterior, only God knew what existed. Later we found how much the little girl hid within herself.

I can still see her standing by her little rocking chair, face expressionless, but knuckles white with clutching the back of the chair in a wringing sort of motion. Mechanically she obeyed her foster mother when asked to show us her new doll. Connie seemed relieved when her foster mother suggested she take Lorrie out to the back yard where there were outdoor playthings.

We relaxed when we heard the two little girls giggling and talking. It was then Mrs. Huff explained to us why Connie was so reticent.

When Connie was about three a Canadian couple who had a little boy and wanted a sister for him about the same age, had taken Connie to their home for three days to "Try her out." I suppose the mother could not have any more children.

Apparently the boy had been terribly spoiled, and had hit Connie with no interference from the parents. "She had bruises all over." Said Mrs. Huff. When Connie is frightened, she clams up completely, even shuts off her emotions, at least as far as they are observable. She can stare at you with a totally blank expression.

After three days in the young bully's company, she was in a state of complete terror. The couple brought her back, saying right in front of her, "We don't want her, she is too dumb. It had taken Mrs. Huff six months to calm her down.

After two more visits, Connie seemed comfortable with us. Her foster mother had had a quiet talk with the child. She said to her "I have been your mommy for four years now, but as you keep saying 'I am a big girl now' these nice people will be your big girl parents."

So it was when we finally came to take her, she was quiet, almost emotionless. She kissed her foster mother, but there were no tears. Mrs. Huff saved hers for later!

After a very slow trip we returned to Mill Valley and immediately phoned my mother. She was so anxious to see our new daughter. The next day she met her and took to her immediately. "She is such a little lady."

All of 1958 and 1959 mama was in San Francisco and we were in Mill Valley, but we saw her frequently. Either she took the Greyhound bus to Mill Valley and walked the half–mile to our house, or we drove to San Francisco. She often kept the two girls overnight, and Russell and I caught up on being alone, or partying with friends.

Adela the seamstress took out her sewing machine, and joyfully made wonderful dresses and costumes for her granddaughters. This was not "work" as was the dressmaking in the depression years.

But as Connie was about to enter first grade and Lorrie Kindergarten there was a change in our lives that delighted my mother

SACRED HEART

The events that led up to a move to San Francisco started with a visit with Connie's Kindergarten teacher. "Where are you planning to enroll her for first grade?" she asked.

I replied "At our local Catholic school."

"Well, I am afraid Connie will not receive the special attention she needs. St Albert's is so crowded."

"Would a private school, like the Convent of the Sacred Heart in San Francisco be the answer?" I asked.

The kindergarten teacher thought that might solve Connie's problem. She needed individual attention.

We couldn't afford the tuition at the convent, but as luck would have it, the nuns had been wanting to add dancing classes to the convent's curriculum. I presented a resume stating my experience with Arthur Murray and Covey School where I had taught interpretive dancing

We sold our Mill Valley house and moved into a spacious apartment on Pacific Avenue, just a block from the Sacred Heart Convent.

For three years I taught all grades and High School. There were elaborate productions. Meanwhile, Connie had special tutoring, but still had trouble with reading and math.

My mother was always interested in the girls, still made dresses and costumes for them. But what of my relations with mama? An entry in my journal in 1961 best tells.

My mother has periodically been the cause of emotional stress. I had thought things were going beautifully. She had always complained that she didn't see me enough, although she lived only twenty minutes away from us on Pacific Avenue. Then she found an apartment on the same block. I ran in practically every day; mama seemed satisfied.

One day she told me she was having a little dinner party; she had invited my cousin Hugh Nicol, his mother aunt Mary and Kay a young lady, Hugh's age. Kay had sublet one of mama's former apartments.

Mama suggested I drop in after dinner to say hello, and laughingly explained that she hadn't invited us for lack of room. As I walked over that evening I thought "Aren't things wonderful now. Mama is having a little dinner party—she is normal and I am proud of her. This is how life should be. I am a grown woman, we both have our own lives. We are interested in each other but there is no clinging, no interference."

When I came into the apartment I saw a neighbor in the living room, but not the girl she had invited. "Where's Kay?" I asked.

Without a word mama ushered me into her tiny bedroom. When I asked again, "Where's Kay?" she said "Shut up" and slapped my arm. I flared up, "How dare you!" and my mother answered with a slap on the face. Again I muttered "How dare you!" Another slap.

With that I exploded, "This is the end! You'll never see me again." And I walked out slamming the front door.

The misery of another rift, regret that I had not been cool and dignified far outweighed my hurt and humiliation at the slap.

Russell said he would be shocked if I called her; I was inclined to agree. If I came crawling back she would lose all respect for me.

But the next day the fire knocked everything else out of the picture.

PACIFIC AVENUE FIRE

I was still at school working on my last show of the school year. Passing by the courtyard facing Broadway I was surprised to see a crowd of students and teachers gathered there and pointing "Fire on the next block!"

I looked and saw the roof of our apartment building all in flames. "That's my house!" And turning to one of the nuns there I asked "Please tell my children to stay here, not walk home as usual. I will be back as soon as I know what is happening."

It was impossible to get into the building. I tried but a policeman pushed me back. Luckily I saw Dr. Wilson, our neighbor. He assured me that Russell, who had stayed home with a cold was all right, "He is in the apartment trying to save things. The fire has been contained on the top floor." Later I learned that two little boys had thrown a cigarette they were smoking down the garbage shoot, when they heard someone coming.

So I returned to the convent, found the girls and told them Daddy was all right; our things? I don't know now." They ran off to the chapel to pray.

Next I went across Broadway to assure Grandma Jones that Russell was safe. Then I phoned mama–the slap incident forgotten.

I told her that as soon as I knew what was going to happen I would come over. Meanwhile we spent the night at grandma Jones and the next day contacted our Fireman's Fund insurance agent. He suggested we contact an outfit that takes all one's possessions, warehouses it, repairs some items, disposes of those ruined, and bills the insurance company. He also reminded us that we had coverage for shelter. "Commensurate with style of living." Pacific Avenue San Francisco was top "style of living." We were installed at a luxury motel on Van Ness Ave.

The girls alternated staying with grandma and with Lita after school. I still had rehearsals and final preparation for my last, most elaborate production.

It was a great success, but the Orchids I received did not make up for the fact my family, including my mother did not attend. Instead they were waiting for me at the Holiday Inn. I had invited mama for dinner.

When I returned there, it was to find my mother and Russell on the verge of murdering each other. She had been nagging about the cleaning woman we had dismissed after the fire. She thought the girl should have been paid for the day she missed. Russell had never thought she was any good, and felt he owed nothing. My mother was hoping to stay for dinner, but Russell was too angry.

So I sadly walked her to the streetcar. I wondered if all my life I would be torn between their enmities. Whenever there happened to be peace between them, I would cynically wonder how long it would last.

BUCHANAN

From the motel we rented a flat on Buchanan Street, also near the school. I will not give details of the three miserable years at Buchanan. But two incidents stand out.

Now that I was not working, money again became a problem. Russell would give me $5.00 at a time, never enough. I still had some bills from my teaching days. The $100 stipend had not always covered some expenses. So I had registered with a Temporary Work Agency.

My mother was furious at my working again. "You are bored with your husband, your children, your mother!"

That wasn't true! I just didn't want to beg for money. However I also felt guilty. One entry in my journal shows how I felt.

"I was alone in the apartment. It was so peaceful. I wanted to do three things before going over to mama's at noon; the beds, pick up the children's room, mop the kitchen and vacuum. At 11:30 mama phoned, pathetic, "feels sick." I feel a fury, been enjoying lovingly caring for my house. But I feel guilty and rush over to mama's apartment. But when I asked her, "What's the matter?" She replied, "I feel numb all over." BUT I DON'T BELIEVE HER!" Then in huge slanting letters in my journal I wrote," ALBATROSE ALBATROSE!"

However, I just let my journal see my frustration with mama's demanding my attention. I didn't believe she was really sick. I had other things in my life that were important.

Right now, the most important thing was Connie. Russell and I were in complete agreement on the need to do something about her schooling. She had been held back at the Sacred Heart, so with the nun's agreement we took her out. We tried home schooling with a special teacher, no improvement in her reading or arithmetic.

Then our good friend Jim Hamrock, a principle in the public school system suggested a move to the Peninsula. There is plenty of money down there. Education is a priority so the public schools are excellent. We made the decision! We chose Menlo Park because there is a branch of Sacred Heart there, Lorrie could continue the curriculum to which she was accustumed.

Connie attended Encinal School for 7th and 8th grades, and Menlo Atherton for High School. It was discovered she is Dyslectic. Dyslectics see print as in a mirror. The special instruction she received under the Menlo Park School system cured her. She reads voluminously now.

We moved into a beautiful, spacious garden apartment, with a swimming pool and interesting neighbors. We were there thirty four eventful but happy years.

Both girls graduated and married. Heather was born. There were good times and bad with my mother. Let me continue with her story.

* * * * * * * * * * * *

SEVEN YEARS MORE

Things went well till the end of 1973. We even brought mama down for three days at Christmas. I had the whole family together for the first time. There is a wonderful picture with all of them;

Mrs. Jones, sitting on the blue sofa with a questioning look in her large brown eyes. Next Mark, ever serious, standing behind his mother. On the long sofa were Michael with his mischievous smile and his arm around his Latin American wife, Rosalie.

My mother was sitting in a chair by herself, looking very relaxed and as usual beautifully dressed.

But a couple of months after I felt my mother going downhill; she was not even able to attend to her mail. On one of my visits to the city I found unpaid bills, and even a couple of checks in unopened envelopes. I suspected she was taking more sleeping pills than she admitted. I wonder what I could have or would have done had I known of some letters I found years later. They were from Olga Suhr, mama's sister- in- law in Nicaragua. I quote.

March 1969 – I hope your health has improved, take care of yourself. I hope you wont have to depend on so many pills. These pills weaken you and furthermore cause depression after their effect is gone."

April 28, 1969 – I hope you are feeling better. I was terribly preoccupied when you were so ill and so alone."

July 16, 1969 – I am sending you some capsules called MEGADON. I am told they are the same as SECONAL.

Let me know as soon as possible if you receive them. I wrapped them in a little cardboard as you instructed me. As soon as I know you received them, I will send the rest with Sonia who is going to San Francisco."

Mama apparently took these pills, a few enclosed in each letter, besides the pills obtained from three different doctors.

"Oh Doctor, I just can't sleep. I just need a little help." And on to the next doctor a couple of weeks later.

Russell drove me to San Francisco at least once a week, and though I usually found mama in bed, she seemed to have recovered from the time I had found that box of unopened mail.

She had moved to the Carlton Hotel, where meals were served. I felt a little less guilty knowing she would have people around her.

Later I found a letter from one of the residents who had befriended her.

Dear Adele:

One of the maids told me that a few days ago you fell again; I have been very anxious about you. Each day I think of calling you, but am afraid you might be resting. So I decided to write this just so you would know you are in my thoughts and prayers each and every day. I really miss you so much. I hope you can come down very soon.

If there is any thing I can do in any way please do not hesitate to let me know. Remember you are always in my thoughts.

Sincerely Marie Myers # 106."

Two months later, February 1974, I received a call from the hotel. My mother had fallen and needed emergency care. We rushed up to San Francisco and went straight to Presbyterian hospital emergency. There sat my beautiful, dignified mama, dressed in her padded, black velvet robe, with the red silk lining.

All around her were drugged up teenagers, either shaking violently, or slumped down in a chair.

My mother was admitted, stayed six days but refused to stay any longer, even though the hospital wanted to do further tests. We took her back to the hotel, but six days later made another rushed trip to the hospital. She had fallen again and this time broken her hip.

Her physician Dr. Pillsbury was called and checked her into St. Luke's hospital. He had battled with her for two years about losing weight, doing exercise and doing without the sleeping pills he reluctantly prescribed. He didn't know till a day later that dozens of Seconal pills had been discovered sewn into the lining of her black velvet robe. Only later did mama tell me of the hell she went through when they forcibly withdrew her from the drug.

Dr. Pillsbury took me aside when I visited the third day, "Well now you have her in your power." Imagine! Adela, my mama in my power! So between the doctor and me it was decided to place her in a nursing home until the break was totally healed. Menlo Extended Care, just half a mile from our apartment in Menlo Park was ideal. I went daily, and insisted she get out of bed and walk.

We would walk down a long hall, just outside her room. There were pictures of different cities, and at the end, with great glee mama would exclaim, "I got to Venice!" as she gazed at the last of her picture travelogue.

Though Menlo Extended Care was close enough for me to visit daily, mama still longed to be in our home. Mrs. Jones had occupied the apartment adjoining ours for several years now. The second bedroom had been Lorrie's, but now that she was married it remained unused.

To my surprise and joy Russell suggested we let my mother have the room. I suggested I pay half the rent out of mama's income. But still it seemed like a miracle to me, after the bitterness my mother felt towards the Joneses. She blamed them for having allowed us to marry without her consent. But really, she couldn't be angry with poor Ysabel Jones. My mother-in-law had had a fall the year before. While she was crossing El Camino, a car had gone through the red light. Mrs. Jones had jumped out of the way, but had fallen and hit her head. After that she became increasingly senile. She had to be watched so that she wouldn't wander off.

Russell would take his mother out to lunch and a ride, but mama liked to stay in bed. At about one o'clock mama would have a dish of cottage cheese, with maybe some fruit, the only thing she seemed able to digest. She could fix this herself. I was at work at Stanford Research Institute during lunchtime.

But in the evenings mama would finally be dressed, and the two old ladies would sit in front of the television and eat the meal I brought in daily. My mother would explain the news to her, Watergate, Nixon's resignation, Gerald Ford becoming president and pardoning Nixon, and of course the agony of the Vietnam war.

* * * * *

DADDY DIES

In April of 1975 I received a phone call from Mexico. It was Ivy my half sister. Years ago she had promised to let me know if daddy were dying. She was keeping that promise with this phone call. I asked her to hang on and rushed into mama's room.

"Mama, daddy is dying, shall I go to him?"

"Go, yes go!" she said; the urgency in her voice told me she was reliving her own father's death and her sorrow at not having gotten to him in time. This superceded her bitterness toward my father. My mother did not want me go through the regret she had suffered at not being with her father when he died.

My dear Russell performed miracles in getting a ticket from a travel agent blocks away and some Mexican money from the bank on his way home. Within four hours after Ivy's phone call I was on the plane headed for Mexico. Russell said he would phone the family and give them flight number and time of arrival.

When I got to Mexico and went into the waiting room there stood my relatives, three generations of them. My cousin Ruthie came forward, hugged me and kissed me on both cheeks. She asked me, "Don't you want to go to the house first to get some rest?"

"No. Take me straight to the hospital, to my Daddy."

* * * *

He lay there so still, so pale. Carmen greeted me with a hug and tears. I asked, "Any hopes?"

"No, but they don't know how long." She too wanted me to go to their house; didn't I need rest?

"No, all I want is to be with Daddy. I will stay as long as he is here."

So it was, that entire night I lay on a couch they brought in, never even took off my tall black boots. I would doze off, but periodically wake to hear Carmen murmuring to her beloved Arturito. There were only sounds of quiet breathing from him.

The next morning, we took a chance and went out for a quick breakfast. When we returned, Carmen tried to give my father a sip of milk. She begged him, "Tome to lechita que tanto te gusta." "Take some of the milk that you so love." Then suddenly she cried out "Esta muerto!" I ran out to call the nurse; she came immediately– yes he is gone.

We wanted to stay in the room, but the nurse and assistants brusquely ushered us out; "We must prepare the body, you cannot stay in the room."

"THE BODY!" This is my Daddy, Carmen's husband! Why couldn't they let us mourn a few minutes? But at least my daddy went out whole. They had wanted to amputate his Gangrenous leg, but he died before they could do it.

In Latin America death is embraced, it is honored; the deceased is not quickly buried and forgotten by all but the immediate family.

So I stayed another week through long vigils, when the deceased is never left alone. Then onto the crematorium, where we all sat in the garden outside and watched the smoke rising from the tall chimney. We all gasped when a graceful white dove flew right through the smoke. Each one of us likely had private thoughts of what it might mean.

The next day I was on the plane heading back home, to my old ladies, my husband and my job. Work had become part time so that I could take care of my home duties.

Mama wanted to hear every detail, and we gently cried a little; Adelita for what might have been, I for a Daddy I knew mostly by letters. I keep the ones that didn't get burned to this day.

GRANMA JONES DIES

The six months after Daddy's death I worked only part time at S R I. Added to the usual homemaking activities, taking care of mama and grandma, took all my time. I was able to bring some S R I work home, so I could be with the two ladies.

My mother just wanted time for talking, but grandma we had to watch constantly so she wouldn't wander off. She was as active as a little bird, but more and more confused. It would have been impossible to cope with had not Connie been with us at the time. She was waiting to join husband Ted in Germany.

But finally it seemed grandma's end was near. I quote from the journal I have always kept.

" For about two weeks I have been sleeping in one of the twin beds in grandma's room, because she is so restless at night. One night, when I was trying to visit mama in her room, grandma kept coming in to ask if it was time to get up. I gave her a sedative, and she finally quieted down. The day before I had tried to find what was making her so restless. I asked her if she thought about God, about Heaven. This gentle lady replied sharply, "Don't talk to me about those things!"

But several days later she seemed terribly weak and had spent the day in bed. Words just jumped out of my mouth, "Grandma, are you going to heaven soon?"

She replied, with a twinkle in her eyes, "Yes, but I want you to come with me." My first reaction was a sort of joy, but then I felt I am not ready to face the Lord quite yet.

Several days passed. Gradually Ysabel Jones refused food, and then I could not even get her to take a teaspoon of water. On October 17, 1975 I sat on her bed feeling her carotid artery. Suddenly I felt no pulse. I ran to get Russell, who insisted I call the doctor, because she might not really be gone. When her doctor came he confirmed my own diagnosis.

There was a beautiful funeral presided over by Father Martin Brewer her Jesuit nephew. Family came from all over California, and we held a lavish reception in our apartment complex Activity Room.

But what of mama these last weeks? As usual, sad to tell.

MAMA LEAVES

When my mother realized that Mrs. Jones was dying she phoned a couple who used to work for her. They were to drive her to the Carlton Hotel in San Francisco with all her things. She took me aside to explain.

First she asked, "Mary, do you think Russell would let me live with you?"

I replied, "Mama, I honestly don't know."

"Well, in view of the fact that you and I cannot afford to pay all the rent on this apartment, this is the only solution. If ever Russell wants me, permits me to stay I would return." This last with emphasis on the "permits."

I was unhappy about having her so far again, so after a few weeks made arrangements to move mama to Casa de Redwood, a retirement residence in Redwood City. Meals were served, and the subsidized rent was something she could afford.

That lasted about six months. I had left S R I after Grandma died; I had lost hopes of ever getting anything but typing jobs there. Thanks to my fluent Spanish, I landed an interesting job at Fair Oaks Community Center, as assistant to the director of the day care center. I will just say that it was tremendously demanding; so much so that I neglected mama. She became terribly depressed, again staying in bed most of the day. One evening I received a call from the Residence's manager. Mama had fallen and had to be taken to hospital.

Our own physician Dr. McDowell took charge and installed her at Stanford Hospital, until we could make permanent arrangements.

She remained there a whole month, till Dr. McDowell had her transferred to Menlo Extended Care, where mama had been when she broke her hip and before she shared the apartment with Grandma Jones.

Poor mama here she was back in a nursing home. All she wanted, all I wanted was for her to be in my home.

The facility was just half a mile from our apartment and I went every evening. Only once in a while, maybe twice a week, would she get up and walk. I would tell her, "Mama, if you can't walk I will never be able to bring you home to Connie's room when she leaves for Germany.

For six months, until Connie did leave in June of 1976 I tried. During the good weather I often took her out in a wheelchair and sometimes when I was baby sitting Heather, we would wheel to the playground so she could watch her great grandchild having fun with other children. Mama had transferred all the love she had for Lorrie to Heather. Lorrie had neglected her grandmother, had not even visited when I paid her to do so when I was working so hard at the childcare facility.

That job I finally left because my heart was beginning to palpitate. The duties were just too demanding in addition to my other concerns.

I had my degree in Social Service, and I was finally offered work that used my training.

The job was with Vista, a program that did the same projects as Peace Corps, but was limited to the United States. Volunteers were sent all over the states, to slums, to rural locations with minimum conveniences. We from Menlo Park felt ashamed to compare the easy time we would have with the hardships the other volunteers would face. Most of them were in their early twenties, we were older, appropriate seeing we would be serving "MOBILITY IMPAIRED SENIORS." But we all received the same stipend $300 a month and full medical coverage.

After a weeks training our group of four, three women and one man returned to Menlo Park to receive our big vans, equipped to carry walker and even wheel chairs for some patients. Another week to spread the word of our services and get used to our vans and we were ready for our work.

It was very satisfying, I even thought I could include mama. I took her once on a complete route, but she said never again, "This thing shakes too much- I feel like I am doing the driving."

The three year contract with Vista, 1976 to 1978 was finally completed. For a couple of months I didn't work. I could give mama more time and help Lorrie who had been divorced for three years and had to work full time. I was able to help by taking Heather to preschool, then kindergarten.

When Heather finally entered first grade, Lorrie and I enrolled her at Nativity School. It was right across the street from our apartment.

I was now relieved of the long drive to Pre and nursery school. With Russell's encouragement I applied for a job at our local Brooks photo shop. "You have always wanted to know more about photography, why not give it a try." Russell had said.

I saw mama daily, but she only woke up when I came. That is when she started having the curtain drawn almost all the way around her bed and had a lacy handkerchief covering her face.

I still tried to get her to walk; she just couldn't. My dream of bringing her home became impossible. I went to see my priest. He said, "Mary if you had help you could do it. Furthermore, if your husband were crazy about your mother maybe it would work out.

But in view of the enmity between them it would be an impossible situation. Leave it in God's hands my dear."

The social worker at the nursing home totally agreed with Father Davenport.

One evening when I had been in to visit mama, the nurse took me aside. I am afraid your mother has a bad cold, maybe pneumonia. I told her to phone me if there was any change; no matter what time.

The next day was my day off work at Brooks. Early in the morning the phone rang. "Your mother is dying; get here as soon as you can."

I was there in fifteen minutes.

MAMA'S LAST MOMENTS

A MIRROR OF HER LIFE

Mama was still conscious when I arrived. She immediately asked me if a priest had been called. "Yes." I answered. The little Mexican nurse had arranged for a priest from the nearest church;

he was due any moment. When he arrived he had not brought Holy Communion, only the Holy Oils for anointing. He did not think she would be able to swallow the Communion Host.

When my mother objected and said, "Father I want Communion." He replied "But I thought you were dying." She gently answered him, "Yes I am dying, but I want Our Lord in Communion."

Father rushed back to church and in twenty minutes was back.

A look of total peace came over her when she had received.

Father apologized that he could not stay, but my mother didn't seem to care, he had given her all she needed.

Another ten or fifteen minutes passed, then in a strong voice mama said in Spanish, "Mary, ya no aguanto!" (I can stand it no longer.)

The Mexican nurse who had been so fond of her used her stethoscope and said in Spanish, "She is gone."

Mamita had stood all that life handed her,

in peace she finished that life.

EPILOGUE

Not till Russell and I had completed funeral arrangements, a Mass in Spanish at the Cathedral, the sad trip to the cemetery where my Mamita was laid in the plot that she and my father had bought many years ago to bury their three day old baby Maurice Albert could we be alone.

Finally on our drive home on the freeway, just the two of us, I said "Russell I want to scream!"

"Go ahead, no one can hear you."

So I screamed, "Esta muerta mi Mamita–my mommy is dead."

Then finally I was able to cry. In the following weeks life seemed to just go on, but there was an emptiness that comes when no blood relations are near. Russell was gentle and kind, tried to distract me. Then when I had a two weeks vacation coming up, he had a wonderful suggestion. "Why don't you take a trip to Guatemala to visit all the relatives you have there."

Seeing my loving cousins and uncles and aunts brought healing.

May writing this book and sharing my mama with its readers complete the healing.

CPSIA information can be obtained at www.ICGtesting.com
Printed in the USA
BVOW030725041111

275220BV00002B/5/P

9 781456 738952